mathematics

FOR LEARNING

The Mystery of the Meter

Decimals

Bill Jacob

John Michael Siegfried

Catherine Twomey Fosnot

Heinemann
361 Hanover St.
Portsmouth, NH 03801
www.heinemann.com

Houghton Mifflin Harcourt
222 Berkeley Street
Boston, MA 02116
www.hmhco.com

ISBN 13: 978-0-325-01027-4
ISBN 10: 0-325-01027-7

ISBN 13: 978-0-15-360580-2
ISBN 10: 0-15-360580-4

"Dedicated to Teachers" is a trademark of
Greenwood Publishing Group, Inc.

The development of a portion of the material described within was supported in part
by the National Science Foundation under Grant No. 9911841. Any opinions, findings,
and conclusions or recommendations expressed in these materials are those of the
authors and do not necessarily reflect the views of the National Science Foundation.

Library of Congress Cataloging-in-Publication Data
CIP data is on file with the Library of Congress

Printed in the United States of America on acid-free paper

6 7 8 9   MP   24 23 22 21

January 2021 Printing

Acknowledgements

Photography

Herbert Seignoret
Mathematics in the City, City College of New York

David Stirling

Schools featured in photographs

The Muscota New School/PS 314 (an empowerment school in Region 10), New York, NY
Independence School/PS 234 (Region 9), New York, NY
Fort River Elementary School, Amherst, MA

Contents

Unit Overview

This unit begins with the story of Zig—who discovers five mysterious dials on the side of his house. The dials are part of the electric meter for his house. At first Zig does not know this and he sets out to investigate how the dials work. As he collects data (readings every ten minutes), he notices that the hands on the dials turn in relation to each other (since each dial represents a different power of ten). Using Zig's data, students investigate how the dials are related. As the unit progresses, students use readings from the meter to measure energy to the thousandth of a kilowatt-hour to calculate the amount of energy used during a specific time period, and to determine readings on missing or obscured dials, working with place value equivalents.

The unit focus is on decimals, and since the electric meter in this unit represents kilowatt-hours to the thousandths, it can be used as a model to represent decimals. Because students can see how the numbers expressed as decimals increase with time, the meter is a powerful tool for students to use to determine equivalents and to examine how decimals increase and are ordered.

The Landscape of Learning

BIG IDEAS

- Equivalence: the numbers in different place-value positions are related by powers of ten
- Multiplication and division by ten make the whole shift to the right and to the left in a decimal representation
- If the whole is shifted, one can work with decimals using whole-number arithmetic
- The accumulated increase of a constant rate is the rate times the time
- The constant rate can be determined if the accumulated rate and time are known

STRATEGIES

- Counting on instead of removal in subtraction
- Using repeated addition for multiplying
- Using landmark decimals
- Using the associative property to make "friendly" numbers and adjusting at the end
- Generalized use of a repertoire of strategies for whole-number operations
- Using place value understanding to multiply and divide by powers of ten

MODELS

- Analog electric meter
- Ratio table

The electric meter consists of five circular dials numbered zero through nine that are lined up in place value order. As the hand on each dial makes a complete revolution, the number indicated on the dial to its left increases by one (one-tenth of a revolution.) This model was chosen because the position of the dials supports understanding of place value with decimals in tenths, hundredths, and thousandths. In examining how the hands on the dials move as the values increase, students may have opportunities to confront basic cognitive obstacles in making sense of decimal representations. These dials advance in the same way that the mechanical odometers of old cars worked, so exploring this mechanism provides an experience that students don't get these days due to the use of electronic digital odometers.

The electric meter used in this unit measures thousandths of a kilowatt-hour (or watt-hours), while the meters in most homes measure kilowatt-hours. This change was made to enable students to interpret the action of the meter in operating everyday electric devices, such as a refrigerator, light bulb, or television. When students go home and look at their meters, they may discover this as well as other similarities and differences. You can explain that in the story the meter is different, and you can invite students to think about the relationship of the problems in this unit to the meter they have at home.

The Mathematical Landscape

Most students' initial experiences with decimal amounts occur in the context of money, where they learned at an early age to read amounts as dollars and cents. Because many students have a robust ability to manipulate monetary amounts (add, subtract, and multiply), it is easy to assume they understand how our decimal system works. Yet it is not uncommon to find students making statements like "The number 0.27 is bigger than 0.3 because 27 is bigger than 3" or "Since multiplying by 10 is the same as adding a zero, $10 \times 0.25 = 0.250$." If students can work with money with such facility, why do they make statements like these?

One explanation is that students' familiarity with our monetary system is acquired in the social context, where it is not necessary for them to link their understanding of monetary relations with the notational system; reciprocally, "school math" is often divorced from students' lived worlds. This unit is designed to build a connection by using the context of electric meters, enabling students to explore tenths, hundredths, and thousandths of a new real-life unit—the kilowatt-hour.

When students first observe the meter, they will note that its dials look like five clocks, except that the numbers go from zero to nine, not one to twelve. They will also note that some of these dials display numbers as on a normal clock (with numbers increasing clockwise), while other dials go backward (counterclockwise). The reason has to do with the mechanical operation of the meter, for as gears mesh adjacent gears rotate in opposite directions. However, the most important feature of the context is the fact that a dial must make a full revolution before the dial to the left can increase by one digit. This is how our decimal system works, and it is realized in the mechanics of the meter and in how the meter is read.

As the unit progresses, students move beyond making sense of the meter as a representation of decimal place value and next learn to utilize the relationship between kilowatts, watts, kilowatt-hours and watt-hours. This involves multiplying decimals, and again the meter can serve as a model of the operations. Students are probably familiar with the different wattage ratings of light bulbs, since 60-watt, 75-watt, and 100-watt bulbs are common in most households. Students learn that brighter bulbs use more energy, but more important is that the total energy used by a bulb is the product of the power (usually in watts) times the amount of time the bulb is turned on (usually in hours). In this unit, students make use of ratio tables in these calculations.

Throughout the unit, students will need to add, subtract, and multiply decimals. They work in the context of the electric meter, and during the development of the unit we were surprised how often students would reconstruct strategies for operations with decimals that we see younger students use with whole numbers. For example, students would frequently use repeated addition to multiply or would count on for subtraction. We feel that this is part of their development and that one of the leaps students make is the realization that operations with decimals indeed follow the same rules as they do with whole numbers. As you work with this unit, do not push this idea directly because it will be far more meaningful for students to construct it themselves—and they will.

Students using this unit should begin with a good sense of place value with whole numbers; they should be able to add and subtract with fluency and have strategies for multiplication. Students may still be developing their understanding of division and of fractions, and this unit will help them make new connections. It is important to keep in mind that although students have a robust social understanding of the use of decimals in the context of money, they may not have constructed the big idea that place value underlies decimal representation, and may not see how place value connects to the operations. Helping students construct these relationships is the primary goal of this unit.

BIG IDEAS

This unit is designed to encourage the development of some of the big ideas underlying an understanding of decimals:

❖ *equivalence: the numbers in different place-value positions are related by powers of ten*

❖ *multiplication and division by ten make the whole shift to the right and to the left in a decimal representation*

❖ *if the whole is shifted, one can work with decimals using whole-number arithmetic*

❖ *the accumulated increase of a constant rate is the rate times the time*

❖ *the constant rate can be determined if the accumulated rate and time are known*

❖ Equivalence: the numbers in different place-value positions are related by powers of ten

As students construct an understanding of whole-number place value, they learn that a number like 249 contains 24 tens, with 9 more ones. It is also equivalent to 24 and $\frac{9}{10}$ tens if we think of the 9 as a fractional part of 10. These ideas extend to decimals, and in both directions. The number 34.235 has 3,423 $\frac{1}{2}$ hundredths and it has 3.4235 tens. One way to help students notice these relationships is by using the model of the electric meter and noting the number of times the hands on the dials turn in relation to each other. Students will construct this big idea since partial revolutions can be related to the turns of the hands on the dials on its left and right. For example, if an appliance is on long enough to use 0.020 kilowatt-hours, this would show up on the dials as 2 complete spins of the thousandths dial, which is the same as moving from 0 to 2 on the hundredths dial, or the movement of the hand on the tenths dial of 2 tick marks between 0 and 1. This idea is critical in understanding how decimals are ordered.

❖ Multiplication and division by ten make the whole shift to the right and to the left in a decimal representation

Students know that $3.25 is the same as 325 pennies. Since there are 100 pennies in a dollar, this is the result of multiplication by 100. Or if they have 50 dimes, they can divide by 10 to find they have 5 dollars. This big idea links the place value structure of the previous big idea to the operations of multiplication and division. Students will learn that there are 1,000 watts in a kilowatt, so when they analyze 0.075 kilowatts, they will find it is 75 watts, the result of multiplying 0.075 × 1000. Operations like this are so frequently taught by rote that students often do the computation without a clue as to why. The work with the electric meter builds an understanding of the meaning behind the computation.

❖ If the whole is shifted, one can work with decimals using whole-number arithmetic

When first adding money, students may understand a calculation like $1.25 + $2.50 = $3.75 as combining the dollars and combining the quarters separately and then putting the two amounts together. Then, if they think about pennies, they may note it is the same calculation as 125 + 250 = 375 (and often they will calculate the latter using money as the model!). Soon they will realize that if they shift units carefully when working with decimal fractions, all they will ever need is whole-number arithmetic. But they need to construct this big idea themselves by considering what happens when they work with and without shifted units. In *The Mystery of the Meter* students will work with kilowatt-hours and watt-hours, initially using the meter as a model to represent calculation in kilowatt-hours and then noting that whole-number arithmetic applies when working with watt-hours.

❖ The accumulated increase of a constant rate is the rate times the time

If you spend $1.25 per day on lunch for five days, you spend $1.25 × 5 = $6.25 over five days. This type of computation, multiplying a rate times time, is useful in many situations and works in the context of the electric meter as well. Here, the power used by an appliance is measured in kilowatts, so a 60-watt light bulb uses 0.060 kilowatts. If it is on for half an hour, then it will use 0.060 × ½ = 0.030 kilowatt-hours of energy. The accumulation over time of using power is the energy used. In other words, the rate in this case is power (in kilowatts) and rate times time gives energy used (in kilowatt-hours.) This is a key idea needed to solve many of the mysteries involving the meter in this unit, and students will come to realize it by considering the readings of the meter at uniform time intervals under varying circumstances.

❖ The constant rate can be determined if the accumulated rate and time are known

This reverses the big idea that the accumulated increase of a constant rate is the rate times the time. If the reading on the meter increases at a constant rate for four hours and the total increase shown is 0.300 kilowatt-hours, then during each hour the meter increased 0.075 kilowatt-hours. This means that 75 watts or 0.075 kilowatts of power were being used during this time.

STRATEGIES

As you work with the activities in this unit, you will notice that students will use many strategies in calculating kilowatt-hours. These strategies mirror strategies younger students use when developing their understanding of addition and subtraction (Fosnot and Dolk 2002). Here are some strategies to notice:

- ❖ *counting on instead of removal in subtraction*
- ❖ *using repeated addition for multiplying*
- ❖ *using landmark decimals*
- ❖ *using the associative property to make "friendly" numbers and adjusting at the end*
- ❖ *generalized use of a repertoire of strategies for whole-number operations*
- ❖ *using place value understanding to multiply and divide by powers of ten*

❖ Counting on instead of removal in subtraction

This is a common strategy for students in subtraction contexts in the early grades. It comes up here in the context of the meter when students have to find the number of kilowatt-hours used in a particular time interval. The contexts in the unit involve comparison of meter readings taken at different time intervals—subtraction as difference. Contexts like these often cause students to count on. Students also may initially need to use the meter and the spinning of the dials to model the difference as an increase if their understanding of place value as it relates to decimals is not yet strong. Although counting on is very appropriate in the beginning stages of the development of addition and subtraction with decimals, it is only the starting place. As students begin to gain a deep understanding of the place value involved, they need to be encouraged to make use of other strategies they developed for whole-number operations.

❖ Using repeated addition for multiplying

This is a common strategy for multiplication when students are first making sense of the operation. If students need to know how many kilowatt-hours a 60-watt refrigerator uses over four hours, they may use the meter to represent the calculation as 0.060 + 0.060 + 0.060 + 0.060. At a later point, as they construct ideas about the relationships between the place value positions in decimal notation, they may adopt the strategies they are currently using for whole-number multiplication.

❖ Using landmark decimals

Most students are aware that 25 cents is a quarter dollar and they therefore readily recognize that $0.25 is $\frac{1}{4}$ of a dollar. This unit increases recognition of other decimals that involve thousandths. As their understanding of place value in relation to decimals grows, students begin to use landmarks as they compute. For example, in adding 0.096 and 0.036 they might add 0.004 first to reach the landmark of 0.100, and then add the remaining 0.032. These strategies should be encouraged, as they are evidence of an awareness of place value.

❖ Using the associative property to make "friendly" numbers and adjusting at the end

Some students will multiply by 1000 in the beginning to represent all decimals as whole numbers (watt-hours) and then multiply by $\frac{1}{1000}$ to revert to decimals (kilowatt-hours) at the end of the computation if necessary. Other students will work with kilowatt-hours and then convert to watt-hours at the end if necessary. These equivalent strategies are important to compare and discuss.

❖ Generalized use of a repertoire of strategies for whole-number operations

Once students' understanding of place value is solid, they begin to realize that all the strategies they used for whole-number operations apply to decimal operations as well. At this point, students should be encouraged to vary their strategies depending on the numbers just as they do when working with whole numbers.

❖ Using place value understanding to multiply and divide by powers of ten

Students know that multiplying a thousandth by ten results in a hundredth; dividing a hundredth by ten results in a thousandth, and so forth. They are able to extend this to multiplication and division by powers of ten and to understand the shift of the decimal point that occurs, for example that $1.25 \div 100 = 0.0125$.

MATHEMATICAL MODELING

The model introduced in this unit is an analog electric meter. This model supports students in developing the relationship between place value and decimal notation. The five dials model decimal number representation—tens, ones, tenths, hundredths, and thousandths of kilowatt-hours. The model operates mechanically as an illustration of the way in which decimals increase.

Models go through three stages of development (Gravemeijer 1999; Fosnot and Dolk 2002):

❖ *model of the situation*

❖ *model of students' strategies*

❖ *model as a tool for thinking*

❖ Model of the situation

Initially models grow out of representing the situation—in this unit, the model is an analog electric meter with movable dials, and the diagrams of the meters illustrate the situation. The energy used in a given time interval is the difference between the readings on the meter. This can be modeled over time by the motions of the hands on the various dials on the movable-hands dial poster. Each dial corresponds to a digit in the decimal representation.

❖ Model of students' strategies

Once a model has been introduced as a representation of the situation, you can use it to display students' strategies as they explain their thinking. Students benefit from having teachers make representations of students' strategies.

Regular increases on the dials, or the relationship between how much a dial turns when other dials turn, can be represented by the movable hands of the dials. Students also use this motion to model their strategies as they calculate energy use. For example, students may have to move dials forward in three increments of 0.060 in order to understand how a meter increases after three hours of using a 60-watt bulb. As you work with students, describe and model their strategies with the turning of the dials to help them realize the meaning of what they are doing. You can assemble a meter with movable hands by making five copies of the dial in Appendix A, attaching the dials to cardboard, and using thumbtacks to attach the hands on the center of each dial.

❖ Model as a tool for thinking

Eventually students will be able to use the model as a tool to think with—they will be able to imagine the dials rotating and be able to calculate that $3 \times 0.060 = 0.180$ and add this amount to a previous meter reading to find a new reading. Although this is not the main goal of this unit, over time the model of the electric meter can become an important model to support students' work with other decimals, not only those on the meter.

Although the meter is the primary model introduced in this unit, you may find students using other models as well, such as the number line and the ratio table. Some students may create timelines with events (meter readings or kilowatt-hours used) marked on them. These representations enable students to keep track of energy used or to find wattages of appliances. The ratio table can also be a powerful representational tool for modeling the relationship of kilowatt-hours to watt-hours. Throughout the unit it is also used to tabulate the energy used by an appliance over time.

A graphic of the full landscape of learning for fractions, decimals, and percents is provided on page 11. The purpose of the graphic is to enable you to see the longer journey of students' mathematical development and to place your work with this unit within the scope of this long-term development. You may also find it helpful to use this graphic as a way to record the progress of individual students for yourself. Each landmark can be shaded in as you find evidence in a student's work and in what the student says—evidence that a student has constructed the landmark strategies and big ideas. In a sense, you will be recording the individual pathways students take as they develop as young mathematicians. Celebrate their accomplishments!

References and Resources

Dolk, Maarten, and Catherine Twomey Fosnot. 2006a. *Fostering Children's Mathematical Development, Grades 5–8: The Landscape of Learning.* CD-ROM with accompanying facilitator's guide by Sherrin B. Hersch, Catherine Twomey Fosnot, and Antonia Cameron. Portsmouth, NH: Heinemann

———. 2006b. *Minilessons for Operations with Fractions, Decimals, and Percents, Grades 5–8.* CD-ROM with accompanying facilitator's guide by Antonia Cameron, Suzanne Werner, Catherine Twomey Fosnot, and Sherrin B. Hersch.

Fosnot, Catherine Twomey, and Maarten Dolk. 2002. *Young Mathematicians at Work: Constructing Fractions, Decimals, and Percents.* Portsmouth, NH: Heinemann.

Gravemeijer, Koeno P.E. 1999. How emergent models may foster the constitution of formal mathematics. *Mathematical Thinking and Learning* 1 (2): 155–77.

FRACTIONS, DECIMALS, and PERCENTS

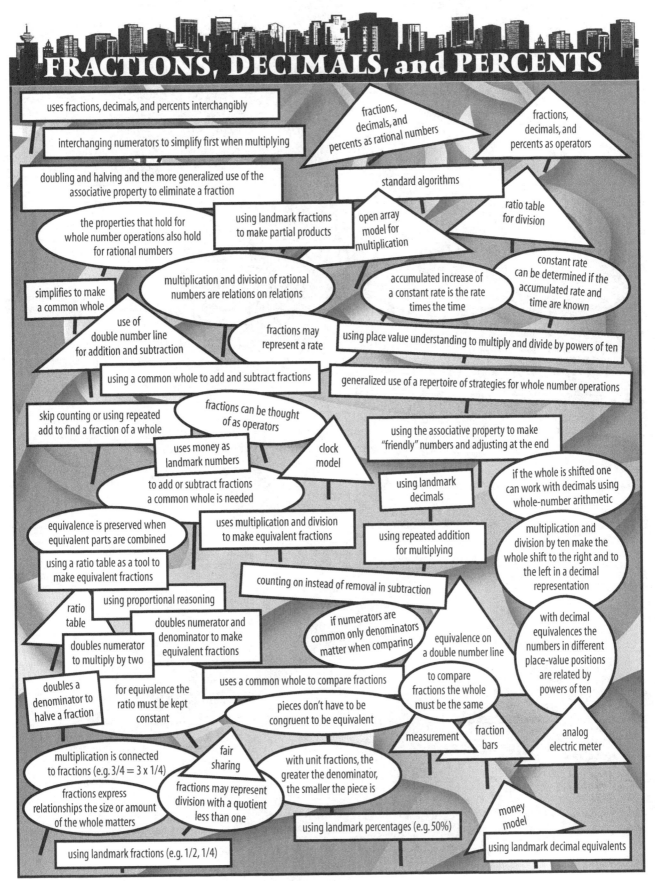

uses fractions, decimals, and percents interchangibly

interchanging numerators to simplify first when multiplying

doubling and halving and the more generalized use of the associative property to eliminate a fraction

fractions, decimals, and percents as rational numbers

fractions, decimals, and percents as operators

standard algorithms

ratio table for division

the properties that hold for whole number operations also hold for rational numbers

using landmark fractions to make partial products

open array model for multiplication

constant rate can be determined if the accumulated rate and time are known

simplifies to make a common whole

multiplication and division of rational numbers are relations on relations

accumulated increase of a constant rate is the rate times the time

use of double number line for addition and subtraction

fractions may represent a rate

using place value understanding to multiply and divide by powers of ten

using a common whole to add and subtract fractions

generalized use of a repertoire of strategies for whole number operations

skip counting or using repeated add to find a fraction of a whole

fractions can be thought of as operators

using the associative property to make "friendly" numbers and adjusting at the end

uses money as landmark numbers

clock model

if the whole is shifted one can work with decimals using whole-number arithmetic

using landmark decimals

to add or subtract fractions a common whole is needed

equivalence is preserved when equivalent parts are combined

uses multiplication and division to make equivalent fractions

using repeated addition for multiplying

multiplication and division by ten make the whole shift to the right and to the left in a decimal representation

using a ratio table as a tool to make equivalent fractions

counting on instead of removal in subtraction

ratio table

using proportional reasoning

doubles numerator and denominator to make equivalent fractions

if numerators are common only denominators matter when comparing

equivalence on a double number line

with decimal equivalences the numbers in different place-value positions are related by powers of ten

doubles numerator to multiply by two

doubles a denominator to halve a fraction

for equivalence the ratio must be kept constant

uses a common whole to compare fractions

to compare fractions the whole must be the same

pieces don't have to be congruent to be equivalent

measurement

fraction bars

analog electric meter

multiplication is connected to fractions (e.g. 3/4 = 3 x 1/4)

fair sharing

with unit fractions, the greater the denominator, the smaller the piece is

fractions express relationships the size or amount of the whole matters

fractions may represent division with a quotient less than one

using landmark percentages (e.g. 50%)

money model

using landmark fractions (e.g. 1/2, 1/4)

using landmark decimal equivalents

The landscape of learning: fractions, decimals, and percents on the horizon showing landmark strategies (rectangles), big ideas (ovals), and models (triangles).

The Weird Dials

Today you will tell the story of a boy named Zig who finds five weird dials on the side of his house. These dials form the context for the investigations in the unit. Although he does not yet know that the dials are part of an electric meter, Zig investigates their mathematical properties. Like Zig, the students in the class study the relationships between the dials as their hands turn. These initial inquiries will lay the foundation for the big ideas regarding equivalence, place value, and powers of ten that the students need for later work with decimals.

Day One Outline

Developing the Context

☀ Introduce the weird dials context and have students talk in pairs about what they notice about the dials and what they think the dials show.

☀ Convene a whole-group discussion of the dials, and record students' observations on chart paper.

☀ Distribute Appendix C and invite students to investigate the dials.

Supporting the Investigation

☀ Students need to construct for themselves how the motions of the hands on the dials are related, so it is important not to tell them how to read the dials or explain to them about decimal notation.

☀ Encourage students to consider the differences in the numbers and remind them that each recording was done ten minutes apart.

Preparing for the Math Congress

☀ Ask students to make posters explaining what numbers they think the dials indicate and the rationale for their thinking.

☀ Plan for a congress discussion that will focus on the relationships among the dials.

Facilitating the Math Congress

☀ To encourage consideration of how the dials are related, scaffold a discussion that will culminate with students comparing parts of rotations on one dial to whole rotations of another dial.

Materials Needed

Weird dials poster, class version [If you do not have the full-color poster (available from Heinemann), you can assemble a meter by making five copies of the dial on page 68.]

Cut out the small hands and place a thumbtack through the center of each, enabling the hand to move on each dial. Set the hands to exactly match Appendix B before you begin.

Weird dials poster, student version (Appendix B)—one per student

Student recording sheets for the weird dials investigation (Appendix C)—one per pair of students

Blank meters (Appendix D)—several copies per pair of students

Large chart paper—one sheet per pair of students

Large chart pad and easel (or chalkboard or whiteboard)

Markers

Developing the Context

☀ Introduce the weird dials context and have students talk in pairs about what they notice about the dials and what they think the dials show.

☀ Convene a whole-group discussion of the dials, and record students' observations on chart paper.

☀ Distribute Appendix C and invite students to investigate the dials.

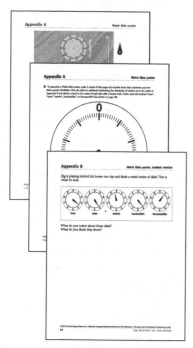

Begin this unit by telling a story about a boy named Zig who has found a weird set of dials on the side of his house and wonders what they are. Later Zig will find out from his parents what the dials do, but initially he can only explore them using ingenuity and careful observation.

The unit begins with students in the same position as Zig. They don't know what these dials are or how they work—they are a mystery. Students are simply shown the weird dials poster and asked to investigate—to record what they notice. Provide students with copies of the student version of the poster (Appendix B) and ask them to discuss with the person sitting next to them the following two questions:

- *What do you notice about these dials?*

- *What do you think they show?*

Pose these questions carefully and allow ample time for discussion. It is critical to allow students time to make their own observations about the meter and to construct their own language about what they think the dials show. Do *not* explain that the dials are a meter or how it works. This understanding will emerge in time as students reconstruct ideas about place value in the context of the meter and think about decimals. If a student recognizes the dials as those of an electric meter, you should note that that is one possibility, but suggest that maybe they are something else instead. In fact, the meter is slightly different from the usual electric meter on most homes and exactly how will emerge later.

After a few minutes of pair talk, have students share their observations about the dials and record them on chart paper. This list will be important over the next few days. Each of the observations becomes a mystery to be explained in subsequent days. It is also an opportunity for the class to develop language that they will need to explain their ideas about how decimal place value works. Common observations include the following: there are five "clocks"; the numbers on the "clocks" go only to nine; each "clock" is missing a hand; some of the "clocks" go backward; there are little marks between the numbers; the "clocks" are like the clocks for different time zones at an airport. [*See Figure 1*]

They correspond to place value.

Maybe the dot is the comma.

The zero and the five are always in the same place.

They look like clocks.

They're missing hand.

It's supposed to be 10, 11, 12, but 0's on top.

2 of them are going counter-clockwise.

3 are going clockwise.

The 6 is not in the bottom center.

There are tens, ones, tenths, hundredths, and thousandths.

Why is the 6 sometimes on left, s.t. on right? (1, 9,...;)

Why is there a dot between ones and tenths?

Maybe it's decimals.

They have a pattern — 9, 1, 9, 1, 9

Figure 1

Author's Notes

Mark: They are a bunch of one-armed clocks with different numbers on them.

Maria: Yeah, but did you notice some of them go backward?

Leah: I bet it has something to do with the cable TV and the channels you can get.

Mark: I don't think so, but maybe because they are clocks, they can find out how long you're watching the TV.

Maria: I think it keeps track of time somehow or I think I heard it has something to do with the electricity.

John (the teacher)**:** Well, I'm not sure we know what it all does, but what about the numbers—did you notice them?

Maria: As I said, some of them go like backward clocks. So I think they are like different hands on a clock.

John: You mean like a clock with five hands? Does that make sense?

Maria: Sure, maybe you have minutes, hours, days, and months somehow.

Lupe: Then the last would be years. But it says tens, so maybe it is ten years and that is why there are ten numbers on the dials.

John: Let's record our observations. There are five clocks, one hand for each, they turn different ways.

Lupe: And they go in opposite ways, first the normal way, then the other way. Three go like clocks and two go the other way.

John: Let's add that to our list: two go counterclockwise and three go clockwise.

Sarah: There are a bunch of little marks between the numbers too. And underneath the clocks it says tens, ones, tenths, hundredths, and thousandths.

John: Hmm…marks between the numbers. That's interesting. About what it says, look again…it says tenths, hundredths, and thousandths. We've listed some interesting things to think about, and it might help to think about the relationships between the clocks …that might be a good start for us. Maria's idea about different units of time might be a conjecture we could test, too.

The students make typical observations about the meter and then start to speculate about what the clocks are used for.

There are other possible routes students could take. For example, some students may think that each dial measures something different—like different dials on an airplane. This point of view is also valid, and students might be pushed to consider relationships by a question such as, "OK, since they are all in the same box, one thing we could try to find out is why they are all placed next to each other."

John keeps the class focused on the nature of the dials and raises the issue of the relationships between the dials. How the dials are related is where the big ideas of the first week of this unit arise. Maria's idea that the clocks measure different time intervals, although not the exact use of the meter, is valuable because it focuses the students on the relationship between the dials—how many turns one hand makes before another hand makes a turn.

An important part of mathematics is to look at how things are related—how a change in one thing is related to a change in another. John has succeeded in getting initial observations recorded and now he will guide the students to proceed with the investigation.

Behind the Numbers

The numbers in this beginning investigation have been selected to highlight certain relationships. They are: 35.961, 35.986, 36.011, 36.036, and 36.061. The values indicated by the dials increase by a constant amount, (by 0.025) over each ten-minute period. Do not expect students to consider this as $\frac{25}{1000}$ and do not push them to use decimal language. Just encourage them to describe the changes of the hands on the dials. For example, over the first ten minutes, the hundredths hand seems to move up from near the 6 to half way between the 8 and 9. Let students count the numbers between the first and second locations of the hand on each dial. Students may think that these dials are part of a large clock, and this theory is quite reasonable at this point. It is also a useful theory because it gets students to focus on the relationships among the dials.

As students discover that one rotation of a dial causes the value on the dial on its left to increase by one number, or one-tenth of a revolution, they are grappling with two big ideas that are necessary for their understanding of decimal fractions: the ideas of part-whole relations and equivalence. Their understanding of these initial big ideas will guide them to increasing facility with decimals as they work through this unit.

Another primary goal of this initial investigation is to enable students to construct language through which they can discuss the dials. This vocabulary builds upon the chart begun in the opening discussion. More observations can be recorded on the chart.

☀ Students need to construct for themselves how the motions of the hands on the dials are related, so it is important not to tell them how to read the dials or explain to them about decimal notation.

☀ Encourage students to consider the differences in the numbers and remind them that each recording was done ten minutes apart.

After an initial discussion and the charting of observations, pose the following challenge:

How could we find out how these dials work? Zig's parents aren't there to tell him, and I think this is a great mystery for us to work on.

Explain that Zig notices that one of the dials has moved a little bit. He decides to investigate. He gets a piece of paper and draws a picture every ten minutes showing where the dials are. Then he studies the results. On the top of the paper he makes some notes. He writes, "I think I am beginning to see how the dials are related." Explain that you don't know what Zig means but you do have a copy of his notes. Assign math partners and distribute a recording sheet (Appendix C) to each pair of students. Ask students to examine Zig's results and see if they can figure out what he means.

Supporting the Investigation

In this investigation, students will grapple with the key ideas embedded in the context: that the rates at which hands turn are related by multiples of ten and that this understanding can be used to determine what the proper reading of the meter is. In effect, the meter is like one clock with five hands (except with separate dials for each hand and with the directions of rotation alternating). To read the meter, one records the highest digit completely passed by the hand on each dial (again being careful about the direction of rotation). But we do not directly teach this in this investigation because we first want students to construct the ideas that underlie the relationships of the dials. By constructing how the dials are related first, students will have a more robust understanding when they begin to work with decimals later in the unit.

Students may need to be reminded that each row of dials in Appendix C is Zig's recording and that the recordings were made ten minutes apart. The time is important. The context of this investigation is structured so that students will see how the dials increase at regular time intervals and will therefore consider the relationships between the dials as they turn. As you move around and confer with students, encourage them to look at the differences and remind them that each recording was made ten minutes apart.

Note how the questions on the recording sheet are formulated:

✦ *How do you think the hands on the dials move?*

✦ *If you were to write down numbers for what you see, what would you write?*

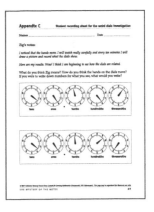

The questions have been formulated in this way because at this point the students should not be instructed on how to read the dials, nor is this the time to explain decimal notation. The objective here is for students to see that a hand on the right moves ten times faster than the hand on its immediate left and to use this idea to determine how to read the dials. In the days that follow students will construct an understanding of how decimals work, but in order to make sense of them they need to first understand how the motions of the hands on the dials are related. As they record a sequence of numbers for what they believe the dials read, have them insert a period (decimal point) between the ones and the tenths numerals. This is *social knowledge*; students won't necessarily do this without your pointing out that the period is written between those two dials as part of the recording, and therefore it is a convention they should all follow. Have them use it because it is written there, but don't try to explain decimals! As you move around and confer, here are some strategies you can expect to see:

✦ Recording the numbers on each dial as a way to determine the change—for example, realizing that in Zig's second reading the hand on the last dial (the thousandths) has moved 5 (from 1 to 6) and the hand on the next dial (the hundredths) has moved 2 (from 6 to 8).

✦ Noticing the tick marks between the numbers and attempting to determine the relationship they have to the movement of the hands on the dials to the right. For example, a student might believe that when the first set of dials reads 35.961, the second dial in that sequence reads $5 \frac{9}{10}+$. The tick marks show the tenths of the unit of the dial. A reading of 35.900 could also be read as $3 \frac{5}{10}$ tens, $5 \frac{9}{10}$ ones, 9 tenths, 0 hundredths, 0 thousandths (if a student believes that each dial is recorded separately and also looks at the tick marks and records them as well). As you confer with students, support them in examining the relationships among the dials. They will learn to record one number for the meter shortly.

✦ Deciding to write the numbers in a column, like this:

35.961
35.986
36.011
36.036
36.061

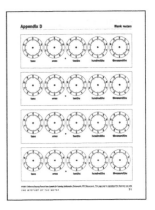

Students might then notice the sequence of the digits appearing vertically, and attempt to continue the sequence in order to examine what happens with the hands on the second and third dials—when will the hand pointing to 0 on the third dial point to 1 and when will the hand pointing to the 6 on the second dial point to 7? Provide students with pictures of blank meters (Appendix D) so they can continue the sequence if they wish.

Conferring with Students at Work

Author's Notes

Maria: The first row of clocks is 3 6 0 6 1.

Lucy: I'm not sure. Why is the third number a 0 and not a 9? It's in between the two numbers.

Maria: Yeah, but then we don't know what any of them are. If we don't call it zero, what do we call it? What do we do? Can you help us?

John (the teacher)**:** Maybe you should talk about how you think the hands move.

Maria: You mean like if they were a clock?

John: That's a good start.

Lucy: But in a clock there are two hands but the hour hand goes a lot slower between the numbers.

John: Think about that. Are the hands ever in between numbers? I'll check back with you a bit later.

(John moves on to confer with another pair of students.)

Alain: *(Addressing John.)* We're talking about all the little lines between the numbers. They must do something.

Toni: Like they're there to confuse us.

Alain: No, really, I think there are two numbers on each clock. They just didn't put all the lines on.

Toni: Oh, I get it, the first row of clocks reads, let's see, 35, 59, 96, 61, and 10. That's a lot of time zones.

John: It seems that some of the digits are repeating.

Alain: Yeah. The last number is the first.

John: That's interesting. Where was the hand pointing on the second dial when it was 9 on the third dial?

Alain: It was almost on the 6…like on the little ninth mark…9 out of 10 of the little marks.

John: And then when the third dial went to 0 and the second one went to 6? *(Referring to the third row, 36.011.)*

Toni: Oh…now it is right on the 6…just about.

As John confers, he pays attention to whether students read one dial at a time or if they examine them collectively across the meter. Maria and Lucy are initially considering each dial separately. John encourages them to think about how the clocks are related and about the positions between the numbers.

Sometimes the best way to confer is to support students to determine a way to start and then to let them explore on their own. John suggests thinking about the movement of the hands like on a clock and then he leaves the students to continue reflecting. Implicitly his action says, "I trust you to work on this and to figure it out." If John had stayed there, it is quite likely the students would have kept relying on him, requesting that he answer their questions.

John uses a question to encourage continuing reflection on the relationship among the dials.

continued on next page

continued from previous page

John: Hmmm…that's interesting, isn't it? If you were Zig, do you think you could figure out what the dials might say if you kept looking for more ten-minute intervals? I wonder when the 6 will almost be on the 7? What would the other dials have to read to make that happen?

By encouraging Toni and Alain to continue the pattern of the change every ten minutes, John focuses them directly on the relationship among the dials.

The numbers indicated on the dials increase by equal amounts every ten minutes. As students record they may not realize this, especially because of the ambiguity of what to record when dial hands are between numbers. Many students will select the number closest to the marker. Listen for conversations about this choice—these may be good clues for groups to share in the math congress. If students always choose the closest number, don't press them to change during the inquiry; instead, make a note to be sure they raise this issue during the congress. Sorting this out is crucial for their development.

Preparing for the Math Congress

Distribute a sheet of large chart paper to each pair of students and ask them to prepare a poster listing the numbers that they believe the dials indicate and explaining why they read the meter in this way. Rather than having students draw figures of meters repeatedly, provide students with multiple copies of the blank meters (Appendix D) so they can concentrate on placing hands on the dials. As students work on their posters, think about how you will structure the congress.

☀ Ask students to make posters explaining what numbers they think the dials indicate and the rationale for their thinking.

☀ Plan for a congress discussion that will focus on the relationships among the dials.

Tips for Structuring the Math Congress

It is helpful to choose two or three pairs of students to share during the congress. Ask them to share their work one at a time and use the work as the focus of discussion. Keep in mind that the purpose of this math congress is for students to have a conversation about the movements of the hands on the dials—the relationships between the dials. Some students may have correct numerical recordings but may not be able to explain why they chose the lower number when the arrow was between numbers. Such a pair might be good to start with because you can prompt conversation about the "why" with the whole class. Those that disagree should be encouraged to speak up. Some groups may forget the rotation reversal and they can be heard as well. Another good choice as a way to begin is to compare two different readings for the same set of dials. This comparison may evoke a discussion of the tick marks and the equivalence, for example, $35\frac{9}{10} = 35.9$. To deepen this understanding, next choose a pair whose work would initiate a discussion of the relationship between rotations of one dial, and how much the dial to the left of it rotates. This topic, with students comparing parts of rotations on one dial to whole rotations of another dial and why they are equivalent, is what the students should be discussing toward the end of the congress.

Facilitating the Math Congress

☀ To encourage consideration of how the dials are related, scaffold a discussion that will culminate with students comparing parts of rotations on one dial to whole rotations of another dial.

Choose several posters reflecting different approaches to reading the dials and explain that since the use of the dials is a mystery, the important discussion is about *how they are related and how they change.* As students present their theories, they will need to justify their reasoning. An important issue will be whether students record the number closest to where the hand is pointing or if they round up or down.

Some students will record the dial readings by writing down the digit closest to the pointer. This issue should come up in the congress. The notion that the dials are some sort of a clock is useful, and during the investigation students might ask if this is what happens on a clock. How does the position of the hand determine the hour? This way they can consider the question of the relationship between the rotation of the hands on the dials and the tick marks.

A Portion of the Math Congress

John (the teacher): Edgar and Rhonda, tell us what you think the first dial reads.

Edgar: Well, I thought the first one read 36.061, but Rhonda disagreed. She thought it read 35.961.

Rhonda: See, on this third dial, it looks like it's on the 0, but it's not quite there yet. I was thinking that they work like clocks, so since it's not quite on the 0 yet, it should count as a 9.

Edgar: I still think it's a 0, though.

John: Rhonda, can you maybe explain more?

Rhonda: Like on a clock, if it was 2:30, then the hour hand would be between the 2 and the 3. Since it's not quite on the 3 yet, the hour is 2.

Edgar: But there's no minute hand.

John: Hmm, that is confusing, isn't it? It seems we have some questions about what to do here. Sasha, you and Carmen started off recording in a different way. Would you share next? Tell us what you did.

Sasha: We saw that the dials had smaller marks between the numbers, so we looked at where the hand was pointing. In the first dial, it's past the 3 and on the fifth mark, so we recorded the first dial as 35.

Carmen: We kept doing that and got 35, 59, 96, 61, 10.

continued on next page

Author's Notes

During the congress, John focuses the discussion not only on what any one given dial reads, but also on how the dials relate to each other. Many of the students may still be seeing the dials as separate entities, not as part of a single reading.

It's to be expected at this point that different groups will have conflicting readings. John uses these as a way to encourage discussion of the relationships. Conflicting readings can engender disequilibrium and provide for a rich discussion.

John acknowledges the confusion and asks Sasha and Carmen to share next. Their readings are quite different. Comparing conflicting readings encourages students to examine relationships.

continued from previous page

John: Did you notice any pattern in your numbers?

By asking about patterns, John reinforces that mathematicians look for patterns. They investigate them and wonder why they are occurring.

Sasha: It was weird. The second digit in one number was the first digit in the next.

Carmen: That kept happening, but we couldn't figure out why.

Sam: The name under the first dial says tens. Maybe the little black marks are like for fractions or something. I think Rhonda is right. It should be 3. I think it is like $3\frac{1}{2}$ or something like that.

Focusing on the relationships with amounts they understand, like tens, helps students begin to see possible connections between the dials.

John: Turn to the person next to you and talk about what Sam said. What are your thoughts about these little marks? *(Allows time for pair talk.)* Sasha?

Pair talk heightens reflection and implicitly says this is an important idea for all to consider as a community.

Sasha: Yeah, I think Sam is right. So $3\frac{1}{2}$ tens would be 35!

Equivalence is now at the heart of the discussion.

Rhonda: I agree, too. See…it is like a clock. You wouldn't say four o'clock, you would say three and some minutes. I think the little marks are sort of like minutes.

John: So let's look at Carmen and Sasha's chart again. You have 59 for the second dial. What are you thinking now?

Carmen: Maybe it is 5 and $\frac{9}{10}$? Maybe that is why it's also 5.9, like Rhonda said. I don't know…I'm not sure. But I don't think we should write a 6. I disagree with Edgar.

Allowing students to disagree with each other is valuable as it pushes them to develop reasons for their assertions.

Assessment Tips

It is easy in mathematics for students to figure out a useful rule and apply it without understanding the deep connections behind the rule. Watch for students who may have reduced the day's investigation to the rule that you always choose the lower number in reading a dial, and ensure that they are thinking about the motion of the hand on the dial to the right of the one being read, and how that right-hand dial requires a full revolution to move the dial on its left one-tenth of a revolution.

Reflections on the Day

Today students investigated five mysterious dials and how they changed after ten-minute intervals. The important issue that students are considering is the relationship between the dials as they move. These relationships form the basis for the development of two big ideas: (1) equivalence, and (2) how the wholes shift in decimal representations under multiplication and division by tens. These ideas underlie the concept of place value needed to understand decimals. As the unit progresses, these ideas will be explored more deeply.

Moving the Hands on the Dials

Materials Needed

Weird dials poster (or the meter assembled on Day One)

Copies of the single dial on page 68, thumbtacks, and cardboard—one set of materials per pair of students

Student recording sheet for the moving hands investigation (Appendix E)—one per pair of students

Large chart paper—one sheet per pair of students

Markers

This session begins with a discussion of what happens to adjacent dial hands when one hand spins all the way around. Many questions about this relationship are considered; they help students to comprehend more deeply place value involving decimals. At the same time, this activity ensures that all students understand the method of recording a decimal from the dials.

Day Two Outline

Developing the Context

* Ask students to talk with each other about how they think the dials move. Then re-convene the whole group and ask a few students to move the hands on the dials to demonstrate their thinking.

* Ask students to investigate the questions in Appendix E.

Supporting the Investigation

* As students work, pose questions that will help them see how the hands on the dials turn in relation to each other.

Preparing for the Math Congress

* Ask students to make posters of their work. As they work, look for a few posters that will help you focus the congress discussion on the relationships among the dials and among the numbers depicted.

Facilitating the Math Congress

* Facilitate a congress that will encourage students to generalize the relationships they notice.

Developing the Context

Display the weird dials poster (or the meter assembled on Day One) again and explain that you have been thinking about the dials some more and you still have questions about how the motions of the hands are related. Have students turn to their neighbors and discuss two questions:

- *How would you describe the motions of the hands on the dials?*
- *Does the movement of the hand on one dial relate to the movement of another?*

Do not explain how the meter works. Let the students come up with their own ideas about how the dials change over time. Some students might have a fairly good idea of how the dials change after the discussion on Day One, but allow all the students to express their opinions. After a few minutes, have the class discuss the dials as a group. Have a few students move the hands on the weird dials poster to demonstrate how they think the hands change over time. Allow the students to ask each other questions, such as "Why do you think it moves like that?" Some students may still not see that the movement of the hand on one dial is related to the others. Encourage paraphrasing and discussion and remind the students that the dials look like clocks, so perhaps they act like clocks too. Next ask:

Suppose the hand on the hundredths dial spins ten times.

- *What happens to the hand on the tenths dial?*
- *What happens to the hand on the thousandths dial?*
- *How do you know?*

Discuss the questions and move the hands on the dials as necessary to help everyone to understand how the dials are related. When it seems apparent that most students understand how one movement is related to another, assign math partners and distribute a recording sheet to each pair of students (Appendix E). Also make available five copies of the single dial in Appendix A with hands, cardboard, and thumbtacks for each pair as a manipulative.

☀ Ask students to talk with each other about how they think the dials move. Then re-convene the whole group and ask a few students to move the hands on the dials to demonstrate their thinking.

☀ Ask students to investigate the questions in Appendix E.

Supporting the Investigation

The context of this investigation is structured so that the students will begin to realize how the movement of the hand on one dial is related to the movement of the hands on the other dials. Students should now begin to see that if one hand makes a complete rotation, the hand on the dial to its right will make ten rotations and the hand on the dial to its left will make one-tenth of a rotation. Subtler is the notion that if a hand makes one-half of a rotation, then the hand on the dial to the left will make one-twentieth of a rotation. As you circulate, you may want to pose questions about relationships like this to the pairs as challenges. Be sure they investigate their own questions too.

The development of language for describing the dials continues from Day One and students may be at very different places in this development.

☀ As students work, pose questions that will help them see how the hands on the dials turn in relation to each other.

Simple fractional parts of dial movements such as half-turns can be difficult for some students to describe, while other students may need the challenge of figuring out how to describe 5½ tenths of a turn. As you confer with students, stay grounded in the context and have those who struggle physically rotate the hands if they need to.

Preparing for the Math Congress

☀ Ask students to make posters of their work. As they work, look for a few posters that will help you focus the congress discussion on the relationships among the dials and among the numbers depicted.

Distribute chart paper and ask students to prepare posters explaining their solutions to the questions in Appendix E. The relationship among the dials is the point—both the dials on the right and those on the left. Also the relationship among the numbers depicted is important. As you confer with students, help them notice that the hands on the dials to the right turn faster than the hands on the dials to the left. How much they increase and decrease in relation to adjacent dials is important. This relationship is given by multiples of powers of ten—an important idea on the landscape of learning for decimals. When the tenths dial spins 135½ times, the dial to its right spins 10 times as much (1355 times) and the dial on its left spins one-tenth as much (13 and $\frac{55}{100}$ times.) The relationships among these numbers are critical to developing number sense with decimals. *[See sample student work in Figures 2 and 3.]*

As students work on their posters, think about which ones would serve as useful focal points of discussion. It is *not* the goal of this congress to have all students share. Many of the posters may in fact look similar, so a discussion of all of them would be long and redundant. Instead, use the congress to build an understanding about the relationships among the dials, and to provide opportunities for the class to continue to construct a common language about turns, half turns, and multiples of ten. Support

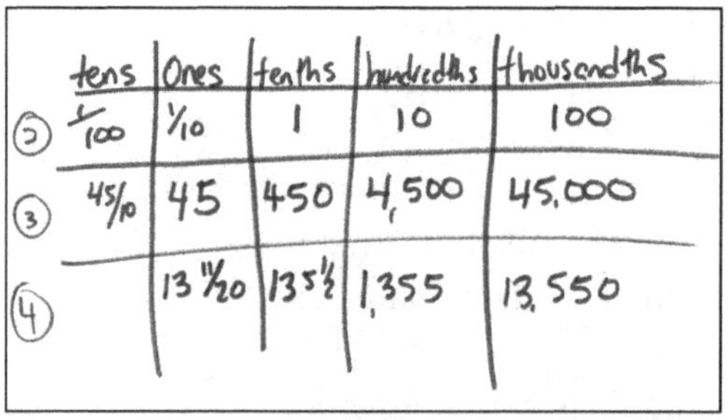

Figure 2

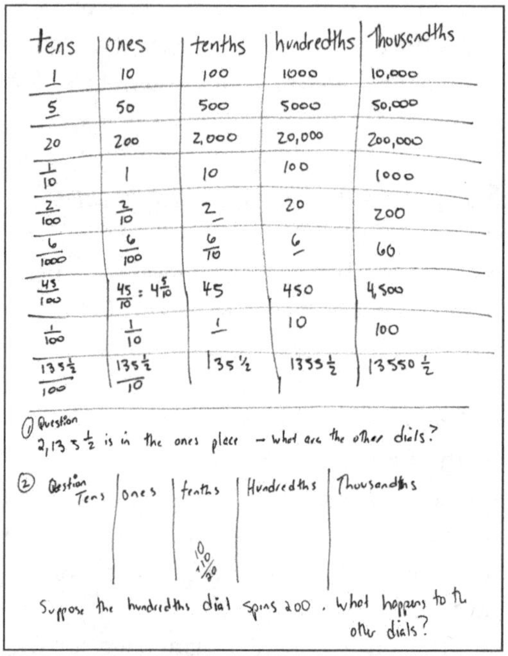

Figure 3

students to realize that the key to understanding these weird dials is multiplying and dividing by ten repeatedly—but you don't need to push them to use the language of decimals to describe it! Stay grounded in the context and talk about the dials. This is purposeful: when discussions get reduced to moving the decimal point to the right or the left, student understanding is short-changed. Make sure that those students who are on the cusp of constructing this relationship are engaged in the congress.

▨ Tips for Structuring the Math Congress

Choose one or two posters that will stimulate thinking about the relationships among the dials. These are not necessarily the best phrased or the best illustrated posters. Instead, they may contain arrows indicating directions and number of turns or even partially formed language about multiplying or dividing by ten repeatedly. Other students may make a chart showing the different numbers of rotations among the dials. How to describe $135\frac{1}{2} \div 10$ would be an important topic for discussion in the congress, so a poster that addresses this may be a valuable choice.

Facilitating the Math Congress

Convene the students in the meeting area to discuss the ideas on one or two of the posters. Rather than having students simply share the strategies they used, focus conversation on the generalizing of the relationships they are using. For example, if a student explains that 45 turns of the ones means 450 turns of the tenths, you might ask what that means for one turn of the ones and how these answers are related. You might also wonder aloud: "I was just wondering how many tens there are in 45. Are there four or are there four and a half? These dials are making me think that 45 is more than just four tens." Keep in mind the multiplicative relationship between a certain number and ten times that number or that number divided by ten. Have students describe these relationships as best they can.

Most students know something about decimals (especially in the monetary context) and may uncover the fact that the decimal point is there to separate the whole portion of the number from the fractional portion. If this comes up, then it can be shared—if not, it will be discussed on Day Three. But don't dwell on this issue. The congress can close with students considering and discussing some of the additional dial questions they posed themselves.

☀ Facilitate a congress that will encourage students to generalize the relationships they notice.

Reflections on the Day

The focus of the work today was to consider how the hands on the dials turn in relation to each other. If a hand on one dial turns 45 times, the hand on the dial on its right turns 450 times and the one on its left turns $4\frac{1}{2}$ times. This multiplicative thinking is the basis of place value.

Reading the Meter

Materials Needed

Weird dials poster (or the meter assembled on Day One)

Student recording sheets for the neighborhood meters investigation (Appendix F)—one set per pair of students

Before class, prepare an overhead transparency of each page of Appendix F.

Overhead projector

Large chart paper—three sheets

Markers

This session begins with students learning that the dials are actually an analog electric meter and that Zig has been reading the meter correctly with the decimal point placed to record kilowatt-hours (so the ones dial reads kilowatt-hours). Zig next travels around his neighborhood to read other meters. Like his they have five dials. However, he needs to develop a theory to read some meters that are partially obstructed or that have missing dials. Students develop their own theories regarding how to read these meters and then investigate those theories.

Day Three Outline

Developing the Context

* Continue the mystery meter story by explaining that the dials belong to an electric meter.
* Ask students to try to read the meters in Appendix F even though some of the dials are covered up by plants.

Supporting the Investigation

* As students work on Appendix F, encourage them to consider the usefulness of the clock analogy.

Preparing for the Math Congress

* Convene a few student-led small-group discussions on the various strategies students used to read the meters in Appendix F.
* Ask students to make group posters describing how they would read a meter if one or more dials are not visible.

Facilitating the Math Congress

* Have students use the transparencies of Appendix F as they explain their methods for reading the meters.
* Be sure the discussion highlights the relationships among the entire set of dials.

Developing the Context

Display the weird dials poster again and continue with the story of Zig:

Zig tells his parents about the mysterious dials he has been studying. His parents explain that he has been looking at the electric meter, which everybody has behind the house. He also learns that in apartment houses, each apartment has its own meter, usually in a box in the basement or hallway. The dials tell how many kilowatt-hours of energy have been used since the meter was last at zero.

Zig's father says that a diesel-electric train uses 5000 kilowatts at full speed. This means that if the train had a similar meter, the ones dial would spin 5000 times during just one hour. That is a lot of energy!

Zig's mother is an electrical engineer. She explains that when their house was built she had the power company install a special kilowatt-hour meter that reads tenths, hundredths, and even thousandths of a kilowatt-hour so they could monitor how much energy their appliances and lights use. That is why Zig's meter has a decimal point and signs under the dials. Most electric meters only measure kilowatt-hours.

Zig becomes curious about the meters in his neighborhood, so the next morning he decides that he would like to read all the meters on his street. But he finds this task more challenging than he thought. There are trees and bushes in the way and he can't see all the dials. What is he going to do?

Distribute recording sheets (Appendix F) and ask students to work with partners to try to read the meters.

☀ Continue the mystery meter story by explaining that the dials belong to an electric meter.

☀ Ask students to try to read the meters data in Appendix F even though some of the dial are covered up by plants.

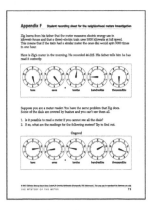

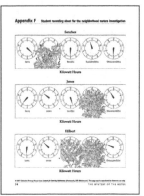

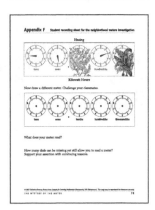

Supporting the Investigation

☀ As students work on Appendix F, encourage them to consider the usefulness of the clock analogy.

The context of this investigation pushes students to further consider the multiplicative relationships between the dials on the meters. At this point, most students will have a good idea of how the meter is read and that a revolution of a dial corresponds to one-tenth revolution of the dial on its left. To what extent these ideas are internalized by students and can be applied in this problem-solving situation will become apparent as they investigate the problem of obstructed dials.

Although the students now realize that the electric meter is not a clock, the clock analogy remains useful during this investigation. The students must now use their understanding of the relationship between the rotations of dials to infer from intermediate locations of a dial's hand the most likely value of the other dials' hands. It may be very helpful to remind students of the clock analogy. This also supports the development of number sense with decimals and relative proximity of decimals to landmarks.

Behind the Numbers

The electric meters chosen for this investigation are set to raise the issue of how the intermediate positions on one dial can be used to determine the value of the dial to its right when it is not visible. The first meter (the Osgood house) can be read as 22.783, and students will have to recall that even though the tenths marker is near the 8, it is not past the 8 so it is read as a 7. The second meter (the Sanchez house) appears as 3_.505, with the tens marker between the sixth and seventh tick marks between the 3 and the 4. The objective here is for students to see that the meter should be read as 36.505 because of the location of the tens marker. The third meter (the Jones house) appears as 61.4_9, with the hand on the tenths dial almost halfway between the 4 and the 5. Although it looks like it may have reached the fifth tick mark, the 9 on the thousandths dial shows it has not quite reached it. So the dial is read 61.449. The last two meters (the Hilbert and Hsaing houses) are each missing two markers. The Hilbert's meter cannot be fully read because the missing locations are adjacent. It appears as 51. _ _ 8. Students may conclude that the tenths digit is 3 but the hundredth value cannot be determined because the ones dial cannot be read that accurately. In the Hsaing's meter, the tenths and thousandths dials are obscured. It appears as 75._8_ and it is possible to read it as 75.281 because the missing information is not on two adjacent dials.

Preparing for the Math Congress

After students have had ample time to work on the problems, ask them to convene in three smaller groups to share their answers and strategies for reading the obstructed meters. Appoint a student facilitator for each group. Join each group for a portion of time and listen in on the strategies being shared. Are they similar or different? Do students agree on the answers? Use this small-group time to allow students to convince each other so they arrive at consensus on the answers.

When it appears that most students have had ample time for small-group discussion, ask each group to prepare a poster that addresses the following two questions:

☀ Convene a few student-led small-group discussions on the various strategies students used to read the meters in Appendix F.

☀ Ask students to make group posters describing how they would read a meter if one or more dials are not visible.

♦ *How do you read an electric meter if one of the dials is not visible?*

♦ *Can you still read the meter if two or more dials are not visible? Justify your answer.*

These questions will be the focus of the math congress. As students prepare their responses, explain that they should concentrate on their description of how to read a meter if a dial is not visible. These should be general methods that can be applied to any meter for which a dial cannot be seen.

Facilitating the Math Congress

Select a few posters and have students present their methods. Have these students apply their methods to the mystery meters on the transparencies of Appendix F. As a class, discuss the students' methods and refine their descriptions as needed. Make sure that the conversation focuses on the relationships among rotations of the dials. Note that some of the subtle points of this problem will be revisited on Day Four when the class discusses Zig's rule. You may want to glance at the discussion there (pages 36–37) because it describes an issue that may arise. If it doesn't, don't force it now; you will get a chance to address it on Day Four.

Some students may think only about two dials at a time and not consider the relations among the entire set of dials. For example, in drawing a mystery dial for 11.999, the hand on the ones dial should be almost directly at the 2 since the value is so close to 12.000. However, students may place the ones hand closer to 1.9 because they believe its location reflects the next digit rather than the *accumulation of all the dials to the right.* Understanding how close 11.999 is to 12.000 is an important piece of understanding decimal relationships.

※ Have students use the transparencies of Appendix F as they explain their methods for reading the meters.

※ Be sure the discussion highlights the relationships among the entire set of dials.

Inside One Classroom

A Portion of the Math Congress

John (the teacher): José and Maureen, you are the spokespersons for group #1, right? Please remember we are interested in a general method to read meters when we can't see all the dials, as well as your answers.

Maureen: If you are missing a dial, then you can look at the dial on the left, and figure out what the missing number must be by seeing what fraction it is between numbers.

Peter: What do you mean about fractions? I don't see any fractions.

Maureen: I mean how much it goes between the numbers. Like here in the Sanchez meter, the hand on the first dial is a little more than half between the 3 and the 4. It's between $6/10$ and $7/10$. So the ones dial should be 6.

José: Actually, I think it's closer to a 7 because it's more than halfway.

Peter: But I still don't see any fractions. Why are you talking about $6/10$ and $7/10$? We looked at the ticks, the little marks, and counted them.

Maureen: It's the same. The little marks are like fractions. If you go around 6 out of the 10 numbers, that is $6/10$ of the way.

Author's Notes

John begins by clarifying that the focus of the congress is a general method, not just a retelling of what the students did. Generalizing gets to the heart of what it means to do mathematics.

continued on next page

continued from previous page

José: You see we have gone a little more than half between the 3 and the 4 so we have to go a little more than half around on the missing dial.

Peter: Oh, it's like yesterday when we saw how far each dial moved when the tenths went around 100 times. They go the same fractional amount as between the numbers.

John (the teacher)**:** Peter, you said your group's method was to count the little marks. Come up and show your method and let's see if we can connect it to what Maureen and José are suggesting as a method. Let's do the same meter, the second one—the Sanchez house.

Peter: Our general method is to look to the dial on the left and count the little marks. This one is between 6 and 7. Since it is not at the 7 yet, we write 6.

John: OK. So it seems like we have two different methods here. Are they related? Turn and talk to the person next to you about this. *(Allows time for pair talk, after which the whole-group conversation resumes.)*

Mark: Well, I think they are kind of the same. Each of the little marks is a tenth…so that's the fractional part that José and Maria have on their poster.

Alberto: Where are the tenths?

Mark: Each little mark is a tenth. In between the numbers are tiny, tiny small pieces of numbers, tenths. That's what I mean.

José: But there are only 9 tick marks.

Mark: No, it's tenths, not ninths.

José: Count them—there are 9.

John: Come show us, José.

José: *(Counts out the tick marks between the 6 and the 7.)* See, there's 1, 2, 3, 4, 5, 6, 7, 8, 9 little marks.

Mark: But it's the spaces in between that matter. Those are the ten equal pieces. So when you get to the sixth mark, that is $^6/_{10}$. When you get to the ninth mark, that is $^9/_{10}$ and then the next number (referring to the dial on the left), here it is 7, is $^{10}/_{10}$. And that is what each mark means.

Maureen: Oh, I get it. The fraction is both places. It's 6 out of 10 numbers on the dial that's missing but it is also 6 out of 10 little marks on the dial to the left.

John: Turn and talk with your neighbor about this. Do you agree with Maureen and Mark? Are these methods related?

By selecting two groups with different methods for determining the position of the missing dial, John provides an important opportunity to compare their methods. When the first group's discussion of the fractional part is compared to the second group's counting of the tick marks, the class can consider the idea that a digit to the right is a fractional amount (based on tenths) of the digit to its left.

Notice how John works to resolve the disagreement between José and Mark. They were counting different things: José, the actual marks; and Mark, the spaces between the marks. This is a big idea of the measurement model— that the "amount" represented by the number is distance rather than number of marks. The electric meter is a form of the measurement model—the motion between the little tick marks on one dial corresponds to the motion between digits on the dial to its right.

John suggests pair talk at critical times to provide reflection on important mathematical ideas.

Reread the description of the big ideas in the unit overview (pages 7–8). Do you have evidence that any of them are being constructed? It is helpful to write your observations about students' work on sticky notes. These can then be placed in student portfolios. You might also want to photocopy the landscape of learning graphic on page 11. Shade in the ideas and strategies that individual students are constructing, according to your evidence. In this way you can map students' journeys as they move toward the horizon of an understanding of decimals.

Reflections on the Day

Today students considered another meter mystery—how to read the meter when not all the dials are visible. Devising a general method to do so involves examining very carefully the relationship of the dials to each other, the equivalence involved, and the space between the little tick marks that represent fractional amounts. Your students are beginning to develop an understanding that the whole shifts when they move the decimal point to the left or to the right in a decimal representation and that multiplying or dividing by ten (depending on the direction) is involved.

Zig's Rule

Materials Needed

Weird dials poster
(or the meter assembled
on Day One)

Students' recording
sheets and posters
from Day Three

Student recording sheets
for the neighborhood
meters investigation
(Appendix F)—copies of
the last page as needed

Zig's rule (Appendix G)

 *Before class, prepare an
overhead transparency of
Appendix G.*

Student recording sheet
for investigating Zig's
rule (Appendix H)—one
per pair of students

Testing Zig's rule
(Appendix I)

 *Before class, prepare an
overhead transparency of
Appendix I.*

Overhead projector

Large chart pad
and easel

Markers

The math workshop begins today with a minilesson focused on several big ideas related to equivalent operations. The minilesson uses a string of related problems to develop the idea that multiplying by five is equivalent to dividing by two and multiplying by ten. Then students review the work of Day Three, solve each other's mystery meter readings, and consider the fine points of a rule for reading meters with a missing dial—fine points that support a deeper understanding of place value.

Day Four Outline

Minilesson: Equivalent Operations

☀ Conduct a minilesson designed to develop the understanding that dividing by two and then multiplying by ten is equivalent to multiplying by five.

Developing the Context

☀ Discuss "Zig's rule" and then ask students to work in pairs to apply the rule to the mystery meters they created on Day Three and to investigate the questions in Appendix H.

Preparing for the Math Congress

☀ Ask students to prepare to either defend Zig's rule, or to suggest modifications.

Facilitating the Math Congress

☀ Discuss the viability of Zig's rule using the weird dials poster. Then have students test the rule using the transparency of Appendix I.

☀ Be sure that the congress discussion ultimately results in an understanding that Zig's rule must be refined to include consideration of the dial on the right.

Minilesson: Equivalent Operations (10–15 minutes)

This mental math minilesson uses a string of related problems that encourages students to examine the results of two equivalent operations, dividing by two and multiplying by ten versus multiplying by five. Do one problem at a time, recording student strategies on an open array. Invite students to discuss the connections between the problems. As you progress through the string, if you notice students beginning to make use of equivalent processes, invite a discussion on how helpful it might be to do that. If the class comes to a consensus that this is a helpful strategy, you might want to make a sign about it to add to a wall of "Helpful Multiplication Strategies." Some students may recognize that this string presents a special case of the halving and doubling strategy they may have previously used. The point of working with multiplication by five here is because of the connections with decimal landmarks.

Do one problem at a time, providing think time. The students should give a thumbs-up when they know the answer. When a student gives an answer, ask for an explanation of how it was arrived at, and represent the strategy on an open array. Ask for other strategies to solve the same problem and have students compare them. Then move to the next question. Ask students how the problems in the string are related.

☀ Conduct a minilesson designed to develop the understanding that dividing by two and then multiplying by ten is equivalent to multiplying by five.

Behind the Numbers

The first three problems provide the scaffold for the string. The answer to the third problem is the same as the answer to the first. The next three problems are also related in a similar way. If students have not noticed the relationships after doing the sixth problem, ask them to examine the problems and consider why some of the answers are the same. The next three problems are also related, and now students have a chance to reflect on the relationships, given the discussion. The last problem has no "helper" problems and students need to make their own—but now they can examine how helpful it can be to divide by two and multiply by ten as an equivalent operation for multiplying by five.

String of related problems:

$$6 \times 5$$
$$6 \div 2$$
$$3 \times 10$$
$$68 \times 5$$
$$68 \div 2$$
$$34 \times 10$$
$$268 \div 2$$
$$134 \times 10$$
$$268 \times 5$$
$$6{,}212 \times 5$$

A Portion of the Minilesson

John (the teacher): Tom, you have 68 x 5?

Tom: It's 340.

John: How did you get that?

Tom: Well, 5 sixties are 300 and 5 eights are 40.

(John draws a representation of Tom's strategy on an open array.)

	60	8
5	300	40

John represents students' strategies on the open array to provide a visual for discussion. He is using the model to represent computation strategies. Over time the model will become a tool for thinking.

John: Does everyone agree with Tom? *(No disagreement is apparent.)* Did anyone do it a different way? Lucy?

Lucy: I did 10 times 68 and then halved it.

John explores a variety of strategies and accepts alternative ideas.

John: Oh, that's a nice strategy, isn't it? Ten-times can be really helpful. Let me draw a picture of your strategy.

	68
5	340
5	340

OK. Let's go to the next problem in the string, 68 ÷ 2. Maria?

Maria: It's 34. It was easy to see half.

John: So can I draw your thinking this way? *(Draws Maria's thinking on a line in order to be able to build onto it with the next problem.)*

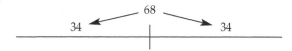

OK, here's the next one. What about 34 x 10? Ricardo?

Ricardo: It's the same again—340. I think it's like halving and doubling.

continued on next page

continued from previous page

John: Can you say more about that?

Ricardo: Well, the 10 is 2 fives. So it's the same. I mean 68 times 5 is half of 68 times 10.

John: So if I draw this, does it show what you mean?

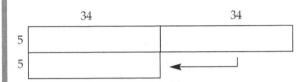

Ricardo: Yeah. It's like the box above but cut in half and then stuck on the bottom.

John: So let's stop and reflect for a minute. Ricardo says some of the answers are the same. Who can tell us in your own words what Ricardo is talking about? Sam?

Sam: The first and third problems, and the fourth and sixth…doubling and halving…that's what he means.

John: So are you saying that a fast way to multiply by 5 is to halve the number and multiply by 10? Let's try some more problems and think about that. *(The next three problems are discussed and then John writes the last problem of the string.)* Emily?

Emily: 31,060!

John: And how did you know 6212 x 5 = 31,060 so fast?

Emily: Because it's easy to see that half of 6212 is 3106!

Tina: We've done this before when we did halving and doubling. It's the same thing.

Maureen: What do you mean?

Tina: Remember, if you want to multiply 18 times 4 it's the same as 9 times 8 because you halve the 18 and double the 4. It's a really good strategy here because multiplying by 5 is easy if you divide by 2 first, then multiply by 10.

John does not clarify Ricardo's thinking for the class. Instead, he asks Ricardo to clarify. Implicitly he is emphasizing that mathematicians explain to the community.

At this point John asks for reflection on patterns in the string.

Although students may have done work on doubling and halving, they may not think to use it with five-times.

Students might not think to halve first and then multiply. Multiplying by ten and then halving is a bit messier when numbers are large.

Developing the Context

☀ Discuss "Zig's rule" and then ask students to work in pairs to apply the rule to the mystery meters they created on Day Three and to investigate the questions in Appendix H.

Begin by revisiting the rules the class developed on Day Three for reading meters with an obscured dial. Display the transparency of Zig's rule (Appendix G), explaining that Zig made a rule, too. Zig's rule says:

First, for each dial where you can see the hand, write down the greatest number that the hand has just passed. Make sure you go in the correct direction! If you can't see the number, leave a blank space. To fill in the blank, look at the dial on the left and count the number of dashes from its number until they come up to the hand. Put that number in the blank space.

Have students look over their work from Day Three. The last question on Appendix F asked them to make up their own mystery meters. Have a student share one and as a class try out Zig's rule to ensure that everyone understands it. Then assign math partners and have them try out Zig's rule for the mystery meters they created on Day Three. Have extra copies of the last page of Appendix F available in case students want to make more mystery meters. Students challenge their partners to uncover the meter readings they prepared on Day Three as a mystery. Distribute a recording sheet (Appendix H) to each pair of students and ask them to discuss the following questions:

- *Is Zig's rule a good rule for reading meters that have hidden dials?*

- *Is it similar to the rules considered in class?*

- *Does it need some modifying?*

Behind the Numbers

Zig's rule is good, but not perfect. One problem is how well students can actually read the tick marks. If, in fact, they could read the marks perfectly, then it might be possible to say that Zig's rule does work, because they won't reach the next tick mark until the dial on the right of the missing dial has completed a full turn. However, because these marks are so close together, if it looks like a tick mark has just been reached, it might be a good idea to look at the dial to the right of the missing dial to see if it says 0. If that dial is at 8 or 9, then the hand on the dial on the left of the missing dial probably hasn't quite reached the mark. In contrast, if the dial has reached beyond 0 or 1, then the mark has been reached. For example, suppose the mystery reading is 12.3_9 and it might look like the hand on the tenths dial has reached the seventh tick mark between 3 and 4. Is the blank a 7 or a 6? This is a subtle point, and some students may argue that they can see the marks perfectly so they won't be mistaken. In this case it should appear that the hand is just before the 7 because the digit following is a 9, not a 0! This conversation and debate strengthen students' understanding of how place value is embedded in the meter.

Preparing for the Math Congress

☀ Ask students to prepare to either defend Zig's rule, or to suggest modifications.

Ask students to come to the math congress prepared to defend Zig's rule or to argue that it should be modified. Convene the class in the meeting area and explain that as a group they are going to test and discuss Zig's rule. Have the weird dials poster (or Appendix A) ready with a sheet of paper to cover dials in order to pose examples for testing the rule.

Facilitating the Math Congress

To begin, poll the class. How many have come to congress prepared to defend Zig's rule? How many want to modify it? Ask for modifications first. Listen to arguments and then discuss Zig's rule and work through some examples as a class. After a discussion about the viability of Zig's rule, the class tests his rule using the dials on the transparency of Appendix I. For the first two meters, it is possible to read them as 21.403 and 35.639, but because of the difficulty of seeing the exact intermediate positions of the hands, students should consider the dial on the right of the blank. For the third meter, it is not possible to determine the value of both blanks. The conversation in the congress should include the examples that raised this issue of the dial to the right being between 9 and 0. The congress ends with refining Zig's rule to include looking at the dial on the right. The tens hand on a meter that reads 3_.999 looks to be on the seventh mark between the 3 and 4. But it is not quite there—36.999 is not quite 37.000.

☀ Discuss the viability of Zig's rule using the weird dials poster. Then have students test the rule using the transparency of Appendix I.

☀ Be sure that the congress discussion ultimately results in an understanding that Zig's rule must be refined to include consideration of the dial on the right.

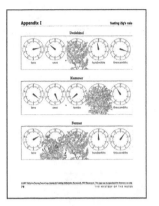

A Portion of the Math Congress

Inside One Classroom

Author's Notes

John (the teacher): What do you think about Zig's rule? Does it always work?

Kelly: I think it does because it's like we talked about yesterday. See, every time one of the hands goes all the way around, the one on its left goes up one number. So, if one of the dials goes from the 0 to the 3, the dial to the left would go up 3 tick marks, since there are 10 marks total…so ³/₁₀ of the way.

Mark: I don't think that always works, though.

John: Why do you say that?

Mark: Well, if you have two dials in a row that are covered, then the rule only works for the one dial on the left. You can't tell anything about the other dial.

John: So you're saying if we only have one dial covered, the rule works fine?

Statements are always examined.

continued on next page

Day Four

37

continued from previous page

Mark: Yes, I think so.

Toni: Didn't we have one like that before where the rule didn't work?

John: Let's try some. *(Shows the meter on the poster. The meter reads 61.4_9 with the tenths appearing to be at the halfway mark between the 4 and the 5.)*

John chooses to have the class read a meter together here as a way to provide disconfirming evidence for Zig's rule. Disequilibrium is a powerful inducer of cognitive reorganization!

Toni: Yeah, see what I mean, you can get fooled and think it's reached a mark when it's really only almost there. If we write a 5, that means it is 59. That 9 is important, too. I think it is 49 and that is so close to 50 that it looks like the halfway point. But it isn't really. You have to look to the other side of the missing dial, too.

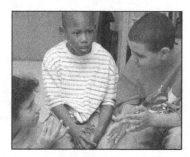

Reflections on the Day

Today began with a minilesson that reviewed the doubling and halving strategy for multiplication in the special case of multiplying by five. Students then investigated Zig's rule and saw that it required refinement to work properly. This examination forced students to think not only about dials to the right or left, but about the relationships among several dials at one time.

What Is a Kilowatt-Hour?

Math workshop begins today with Zig wondering if he can determine the wattage of a light bulb by using the meter. Students investigate the data that Zig collects and find that when the electric use is constant, the meter increases the same amount over fixed time intervals. They find that a 100-watt bulb will advance the meter one-tenth of a kilowatt-hour in one hour. They also work to determine the watts used by Zig's refrigerator.

Materials Needed

Light bulbs of varying wattage

Zig's experiments (Appendix J)—one set per pair of students

Drawing paper—a few sheets per pair of students

Large chart pad and easel

Markers

Day Five Outline

Developing the Context

☀ Conduct a preliminary discussion about how meter readings might help Zig find the wattage of a light bulb.

☀ Ask students to investigate the data that Zig collects in Appendix J.

Supporting the Investigation

☀ Work with students to ensure they understand how the meters work.

☀ Ask questions that will help students focus on the amount the value shown on a meter increases as opposed to the numbers it reads.

☀ Ask questions that will highlight that the amount of increase is constant.

☀ Encourage students who are familiar with ratio tables to use them to keep track of the total increase in the meter readings.

Faciliating a Mini-Congress

☀ Facilitate a short discussion of students' findings for the first few experiments in Appendix J and record their data in a ratio table.

Developing the Context

☀ Conduct a preliminary discussion about how meter readings might help Zig find the wattage of a light bulb.

☀ Ask students to investigate the data Zig collects in Appendix J.

Explain that you have learned more about Zig and then tell the following story:

> *Zig learns in science class that energy is measured in kilowatt-hours. He remembers that he has seen light bulbs that are labeled 100 watt, 40 watt, and 75 watt.*

Show a variety of light bulbs and point out the wattage. Then continue the story:

> *Zig wonders if his meter would register the energy used and if, without removing the light bulbs in the kitchen, the bathroom, the hallway, or his bedroom to read their numbers, he could figure out the number of watts for each bulb. Zig decides to do some experiments.*

Have some pair talk and then a short class discussion of the following question:

- *How could the meter help you find the number of watts of a light bulb without looking at the bulb?*

Explain that you have Zig's data and then distribute copies of Zig's experiments (Appendix J) and drawing paper. Assign partners and ask students to examine the information and try to figure out what it means.

Behind the Numbers

The numbers in experiment #1 increase 0.015 every 15 minutes. This means that in one hour the reading will be 0.060, or 60 watt-hours. In experiment #2, when the refrigerator is off, there is no change registering on the meter, because no energy is being used. Determining that the refrigerator uses 60 watts is one of the main mysteries to resolve in this investigation. (This is because it uses 15 watt-hours in 15 minutes.) It requires that students construct the big idea that governs how energy use is measured, namely that a watt-hour is the amount of energy when one watt of power is used for an hour. So a 100-watt bulb will use 100 watt-hours (or 0.100 kilowatt-hours) in one hour. This means that a 100-watt bulb will use 50 watt-hours in a half-hour, 25 watt-hours in a quarter hour, and so forth. The time intervals designed into the investigation are quarter hours to facilitate this understanding. Experiment #3 shows the meter registering a 0.025 increase every 15 minutes. Experiment #4 (when the refrigerator and the light are both on) shows a change of 0.040 every 15 minutes (0.025 for the light and 0.015 for the refrigerator).

Supporting the Investigation

☀ Work with students to ensure they understand how the meters work.

☀ Ask questions that will help students focus on the amount the value shown on a meter increases as opposed to the numbers it reads.

☀ Ask questions that will highlight that the amount of increase is constant.

☀ Encourage students who are familiar with ratio tables to use them to keep track of the total increase in the meter readings.

To begin, students will have to record the various meter readings correctly. Tour around the class and give their work a quick glance to make sure they are reading the meters properly. If not, engage students in a short conversation to make sure they understand how the meters work. For if they misread the meters they will be locked out of the heart of this investigation (how the meter increases at uniform time intervals) and it is not likely that their further inquiry will lead them to go back and check their readings.

In reading the meters and determining the energy used, students will in effect be subtracting with decimals. Most students won't formally subtract, however. Instead, they will imagine how the hands on the dials are turning to determine how much the value indicated on the meter has increased. The context is designed to facilitate this type of thinking because it is essential to focus on place value when decimals are involved. When necessary, encourage students to use the dials and visualize how the hands turn when calculating how much energy the meter is measuring.

When students investigate experiment #1, they will note that each 15 minutes the value on the meter increases by 0.015. Some may say, "See, it is a clock!" Tell the students to keep working and check their theory. Of course, the meter is not a clock, but this idea is important because it encompasses the fact that with constant power use, the meter will increase at a constant rate. In fact, this is how an electric clock works. You can remind the students that it is an electric meter (Zig's parents told him this), not a clock, but also tell them their idea may prove helpful in understanding how the meter works. You should not tell them they are wrong, because, in principle, they have noticed a big idea.

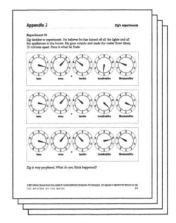

In considering the dial readings a big idea emerges, namely that within each set of three readings the amount of increase is constant. To help students focus on the amount the value on a meter increases (as opposed to the numbers it reads), ask the students how often they think the hands have spun in each 15-minute interval. Then ask how much they think the hands would spin in an hour or in a day. The question of how much the hands spin in an hour is the clue to understanding how the meter can be used to determine the wattage of a light bulb. If students have not considered the effect of the refrigerator, you can ask, how many watt-hours does the refrigerator use in 15 minutes, or in half an hour? If you know how many watt-hours it would use in one hour, that would tell you the wattage of the refrigerator. Students who are familiar with ratio tables should use them here and for those who are not, as they record the data you can help them set up appropriate tables.

Conferring with Students at Work

Inside One Classroom

Author's Notes

(Alain and Lupe are working on experiment #1.)

Alain: I don't get this. What does this mean?

Lupe: Yeah.

John (the teacher)**:** It is a puzzle, isn't it? All we know is that these are the results of Zig's readings taken every fifteen minutes. What are his readings? Why don't you start by recording the readings? *(They record the readings: 28.848, 28.863, and 28.878.)* So are the dials changing?

Lupe: The first three numbers are staying the same…the others are changing.

John: Do you agree, Alain? *(Alain nods.)* That's interesting, isn't it? What are the other ones doing?

John acknowledges the difficulty of the problem but models enjoyment in trying to figure it out. Often students need support to begin and they need to realize that part of the fun of doing mathematics is working through the puzzlement—cracking the mystery, so to speak.

continued on next page

continued from previous page

Lupe: It went from 48 to 63 to 78.

John: So what did the hands do, I wonder?

Alain: I think the thousandths one went around at least once, because the hundredths moved, too.

John encourages Lupe and Alain to analyze the situation by considering the change in the position of hands on the dials. He does not use the word subtract; instead he encourages them to describe the change and how it must have occurred.

John: Oh, that's good thinking! Do you agree, Lupe?

Lupe: I don't know. Tell me again.

Alain: See, if it goes around once, then it would be 58, not 63, and then it must go 1, 2, 3, 4, 5…5 more. That would make the hands say 6 and 3.

Lupe: Oh, yeah. I agree.

John: So let's record that. You said the first three numbers stayed the same and then the difference you said was…

John encourages the students to record their findings, and then extends their analysis to the next set of readings.

Lupe: 15, 10, and then 5 more…that's 15. *(Writes 00.015.)*

John: And so what about here…where it goes from 63 to 78?

Lupe: Hey, that's 15, too. *(Writes 00.015 again.)*

Equivalence is the focus here—understanding the results and being able to interpret them with a variety of equivalencies.

John: So the thousandths dial changed 5 then 5 and then 5… a change of 15 thousandths, or a 1 hundredths and 5 thousandths change.

Alain: Or 1½ hundredths if we look at the little marks instead of the last dial.

John: Right. So what's going on with this meter? Why is it increasing 15 thousandths every 15 minutes? What would the difference be in an hour, I wonder?

Lupe: That's four 15-minute chunks…so 4 times 15 is 60. Would it be 60 thousandths?

John: What do you think about what Lupe said, Alain?

John ensures that both students are engaged in the discussion by asking them to consider agreement.

Alain: I think she is right. But why is it doing this? If Zig turned everything off, why are the hands moving?

Lupe: I think he must have forgotten something.

Faciliating a Mini-Congress

Students will work on more light bulb mysteries on Day Six and have a congress on the relationship of watt-hours to kilowatt-hours. However, it is helpful at this point to bring students to the meeting area for a short discussion of findings after students have had time to investigate three or four of Zig's experiments. Have students share their thoughts about what is happening with the refrigerator and with the refrigerator and 100-watt bulb combination. Ask how much the meter would go up in one hour if only the refrigerator was on. What about how the meter would change in two hours, three hours, or more? How would it change if the 100-watt bulb were on also? As students share their findings and theories, a ratio table for the refrigerator can be displayed:

☀ Facilitate a short discussion of students' findings for the first few experiments in Appendix J and record their data in a ratio table.

Refrigerator					
Time on	15 minutes	30 minutes	1 hour	2 hours	3 hours
Kilowatt-hours used	0.015	0.030	0.060	0.120	0.180

And for the refrigerator and the 100-watt bulb together:

Refrigerator plus 100-watt bulb					
Time on	15 minutes	30 minutes	1 hour	2 hours	3 hours
Kilowatt-hours used	0.040	0.080	0.160	0.320	0.480

This discussion will allow students to discuss the steady increase of the values on the meter over time in several cases, and also introduce them to a ratio table as a convenient way to keep track of the increase. Explain that students will have a full opportunity to discuss their ideas as they complete work on these and other mysteries on Day Six.

Reflections on the Day

Today students investigated another mystery of the meter—how it can be used to measure the wattages of light bulbs and appliances. They noted that the values on the meter increase at a steady rate when the same appliances (or bulbs) are on. In a brief congress they set up ratio tables to keep track of this steady increase and used it to predict larger time intervals. On Day Six, they will complete their investigation and discuss their findings in small groups in preparation for a math congress on Day Seven.

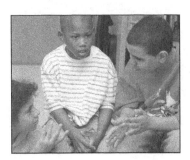

More Light Bulb Mysteries

Today students complete their work on the mystery of the refrigerator's energy use and study a few more light bulb mysteries. Then they prepare their conclusions and hold small discussion groups in preparation for a math congress on Day Seven.

Materials Needed

Students' work from Day Five

Chart of ratio tables from the brief congress on Day Five

Student recording sheet for Zig's second set of experiments (Appendix K)—one per pair of students

Weird dials poster (or the meter assembled on Day One), as needed

Large chart paper— four sheets

Markers

Day Six Outline

Developing the Context

☀ Revisit students' work from Day Five and then ask students to investigate the experiments in Appendix K.

Supporting the Investigation

☀ As students work, remind them that in these experiments, the readings are not always fifteen minutes apart.

Preparing for the Math Congress

☀ Convene a few student-led small-group discussions on the various strategies students used as they investigated the experiments in Appendix K.

☀ Pose a few questions about how much the value on the meter will increase in an hour, and ask students to record their thinking on group posters.

☀ Plan for a congress (to be held on Day Seven) that will focus on the different representations reflected in the posters.

Developing the Context

Display the chart of ratio tables from Day Five and remind students of the work they were doing regarding Zig's initial experiment with the 100-watt bulb and the refrigerator. Explain that they will have time today to continue work on that problem and that you have some more data for them to analyze as well. Distribute recording sheets (Appendix K) and explain that in this set of experiments, Zig tries to determine the wattages of various light bulbs. Sometimes he has the refrigerator on, and sometimes he has it off. Also, his meter readings are not always fifteen minutes apart, so instruct the students that they will need to be careful when they analyze the data!

☀ Revisit students' work from Day Five and then ask students to investigate the experiments in Appendix K.

Behind the Numbers

In the first situation, the difference between the readings is 0.025. This landmark number is used again on purpose to encourage students to think multiplicatively. This difference was the result of readings every 20 minutes—⅓ of an hour. The energy usage for an hour is three times the 0.025, or 0.075 kilowatt-hours— 75 watt-hours. In the second situation, the increase every 30 minutes is 0.060 kilowatt-hours—120 watt-hours. But now the refrigerator's energy usage must be subtracted. This amount is 60 watt-hours in one hour (this was determined on Day Five). Therefore the kitchen light bulb must be a 60-watt bulb.

Supporting the Investigation

As you move around and confer with students, you will probably see several strategies:

✦ Some students will find the difference between each reading and they will need to envision the movement of the hands on the dials to determine the change. As you confer with these students, you may want to provide the weird dials poster to help them. Encourage them to consider the thousandths and hundredths dials together—how the change on one is related to the change on the other. After finding the difference between each reading, they may add the consecutive changes together to determine the difference over an hour.

✦ Some students may realize that they only need to look at the first and last readings and find the difference between them. For example, in the second problem they may write 31.945 – 31.825. As they work to find the difference, you might encourage them to consider using strategies they might have used for whole number subtraction: 945 – 825. You can encourage moving to a landmark number. They might consider how 75 thousandths more is needed to get to 31.900 on the dials, and then 45 thousandths more is needed to get to 31.945. Or you might ask students to consider what the final reading would be if Zig had started when the first dial read 31.800 (since this was 0.025 kilowatt-hours ago, the final reading would have been 31.920 and now the difference can more easily be seen as 0.120 kilowatt-hours—120 watt-hours).

✦ Some students may calculate the difference from the start to the next reading only, trusting from the discussion on Day Five that the increase will be constant. Next they may multiply by 3 if the reading was for a 20-minute period, by 2 if the reading was for a 30-minute period. As you confer, encourage the use of the ratio table to represent the proportional reasoning.

☀ As students work, remind them that in these experiments, the readings are not always fifteen minutes apart.

Preparing for the Math Congress

☀ Convene a few student-led small-group discussions on the various strategies students used as they investigated the experiments in Appendix K.

☀ Pose a few questions about how much the value on the meter will increase in an hour, and ask students to record their thinking on group posters.

☀ Plan for a congress (to be held on Day Seven) that will focus on the different representations reflected in the posters.

Ask students to gather in four small discussion groups and share their strategies and conclusions. After sufficient discussion time, ask each group to work on a poster for a math congress (to be held on Day Seven) on the following questions:

✦ *How can we predict how much the value on the meter will increase in one hour if Zig's kitchen light is on and the refrigerator is on? What about over a day?*

✦ *How can we predict how much the value on the meter will increase in one hour if Zig's bedroom light is on but nothing else (including the refrigerator) is on in the house?*

✦ *What does a kilowatt-hour mean? Explain the meaning in terms of Zig's light bulbs.*

▦ Tips for Structuring the Math Congress

Plan on beginning the math congress on Day Seven with a discussion of different representations used in the justifications. Some justifications may rely on the spinning of the hands on the dials to indicate the changes; others may use the decimal differences from the problem; still others may simply write 0.040×3 because 0.040 is the increase in 20 minutes and 20 minutes is one third of an hour. In the congress, you will want to focus conversation on the relationship among these. Also look for students who observe that the rate of increase for the refrigerator and the light is the sum of their rates individually. Finally, plan on having students discuss how a light bulb may be labeled in watts, but a kilowatt-hour (a unit equal to 1000 watt-hours) is the amount of energy used. It is what you have to pay for, as they will see on Day Nine.

Behind the Numbers

Note that the focus of the questions is on how much the value on the meter will increase in an hour (not what it will read and not, initially, what the bulb's wattage is). The big idea here is that the accumulated increase of a constant rate is rate times time in the context where the rate is kilowatts and the accumulated increase is energy measured in kilowatt-hours. A 100-watt bulb will increase the meter by 0.1 kilowatt-hour in one hour, and the refrigerator and the kitchen light together use 0.040 kilowatt-hours in 20 minutes so they will use 0.120 kilowatt-hours in one hour. Try to keep conversation grounded in the context of the dials. Ask how fast the hands on the dials are turning—are they like a clock? Does the clock go faster if you plug in the refrigerator?

▦ Assessment Tips

It would be nice to place the posters in students' portfolios; however, they are probably too large. If so, you can take a photograph of each poster and staple it to a blank page for your anecdotal notes. Make notes about the strategies and big ideas described in the introduction to this unit (pages 7–9). Do you have evidence that any of these ideas and strategies have been constructed?

Reflections on the Day

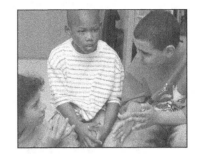

Today students worked on finding the difference in meter readings in the thousandths. Students probably used a variety of strategies, from literally turning the hands on the dials, to realizing that any strategy used for subtraction of whole numbers also works with decimals. In small groups, students shared their strategies and then prepared posters for the congress on Day Seven—where one of the main points of discussion will be the relationship between kilowatt-hours and watt-hours.

Light Bulb Mysteries and the Meter Reader Game

Materials Needed

Weird dials poster (or the meter assembled on Day One), as needed

Students' posters from Day Six

Spinners with numbers 0–9—one per group of four students

Appliance cards (Appendix L)—one set per group of four students

Time cards (Appendix M)—one set per group of four students

Student recording sheet for the Meter Reader game (Appendix N)—one per pair of students

Large chart pad and easel

Markers

Math workshop today begins with a congress on the light bulb mysteries. The conversation is on the following questions: (1) How can we predict how much the value on the meter will increase in one hour if Zig's kitchen light is on and the refrigerator is on? What about over a day? (2) How can we predict how much the value on the meter will increase in one hour if Zig's bedroom light is on but the refrigerator is off? (3) What does a kilowatt-hour mean?

An important focus of the congress is the relationship between kilowatt-hours and watt-hours. After the math congress, the game Meter Reader is introduced and students play in groups of four.

Day Seven Outline

Facilitating the Math Congress

☀ Facilitate a congress focused on the relationships between the different representations students used to determine how much the value on the meter will increase in an hour. Also discuss the relationship between watts and kilowatt-hours.

Developing the Context

☀ Model how to play Meter Reader.

☀ Use the different sets of cards to differentiate instruction as necessary.

Facilitating the Math Congress

Convene students for a math congress. Display all four group posters and ask students to consider the different representations used in the justifications. Some justifications may rely on the spinning of the dial hands to indicate the changes; others may use the decimal differences from the problem; still others may simply use 0.040 × 3 because 0.040 is the increase in 20 minutes and 20 minutes is ⅓ of an hour. Focus conversation on the relationship between the justifications. Then move to a discussion on the relationship between watt-hours and kilowatt-hours.

☀ Facilitate a congress focused on the relationships between the different representations students used to determine how much the value on the meter will increase in an hour. Also discuss the relationship between watts and kilowatt-hours.

Inside One Classroom

A Portion of the Math Congress

John (the teacher): So we have had an interesting conversation on the different representations and justifications on the posters. Let me shift the conversation a little now. Let's talk about watt-hours and kilowatt-hours. What are they? How are they related?

Toni: I think the meter is reading kilowatt-hours. And that's 1000 times as big as the watt-hours.

Sam: But this is so confusing. Because the meter has little numbers…sort of like fractions…but they're in tens, sort of…well, like tenths, hundredths, and thousandths. Those numbers are too little to be 1000 times the watt-hours.

Emily: It's like if it's 1 watt-hour, it's ¹⁄₁₀₀₀ of a kilowatt-hour…because the kilowatt-hour is so big.

John: Let's make a t-chart and look at this. You said 1000 watts were 1 kilowatt, right? I'll write that. So what about 1 watt? Sam?

Sam: Oh, yeah…I get it. It is worth one over a thousand.

John: On the meter that would read one-thousandth.
(Continues to build a ratio table on the t-chart with the class.)

Watt-hours	Kilowatt-hours
1000	1
1	¹⁄₁₀₀₀ or 0.001
10	¹⁄₁₀₀ or 0.010
100	¹⁄₁₀ or 0.100

Author's Notes

John focuses the conversation on the relationship between watt-hours and kilowatt-hours.

By introducing the t-chart here, John provides a visual model and supports the use of proportional reasoning.

Developing the Context

☀ Model how to play Meter Reader.

☀ Use the different sets of cards to differentiate instruction as necessary.

After the math congress, introduce the Meter Reader game. Ask students to form a circle and choose three to play with you as you demonstrate the game.

▦ Object of the Game

The objective of the Meter Reader game is to determine the number of hours an appliance must have been on, based on the amount of electricity used; *or* to figure out the wattage of the appliance, given the time it was on and the amount of electricity used.

▦ Directions for Playing Meter Reader

Students play in groups of four—two pairs of two. One pair acts as the "customers" and the other acts as the "meter readers." A spinner and two decks of cards are needed: appliance cards (Appendix L) and time cards (Appendix M). The decks are turned face down. One student spins five times; the results are recorded on the recording sheet (Appendix N) respectively as tens, ones, tenths, hundredths, and thousandths (of kilowatt-hours). For example, if the spins are 2, 5, 0, 9, and 2, this would be recorded as 25.092. This recording is the initial meter reading for the first round. *Both pairs should record this number.* The customers play first. One customer draws an appliance card; the other draws a time card. The appliance cards show an appliance and a wattage. The time cards show an amount of time. The customers must figure out what the new meter reading would be after that appliance was on for that amount of time. They record it on a recording sheet. They show the meter readers the result and tell *either* the appliance's wattage *or* the time it was used, but not both. It is then the job of the meter readers to figure out the missing piece of information. When they arrive at an answer, all four students check their answers. The meter readers get a point if they have correctly determined the missing piece of information. If the customers have calculated the reading incorrectly for their cards, the round is thrown out and a new round is begun. The pairs then change roles. The game continues until one pair gets five (or any pre-set amount of) points.

Differentiating Instruction

Some students may need to physically move the hands on the meter in order to play the game. The weird dials poster with the movable hands (or Appendix A) can be used as a support if needed. The game comes with three sets of cards: S1 (easy) cards, S2 (moderate) cards, and S3 (difficult) cards. (You might find it helpful to copy the sets on different colored paper to avoid mixing them up.) Students should start with the easiest cards and then add in the difficult ones as they progress. Students can also make up their own cards if they wish. For a greater challenge, customers can pull more than one pair of cards at a time. The game continues as above, except the customers have to figure out the final reading if all the appliances on those cards were on. The customers then give the meter readers all but one piece of information. As before, the meter readers try to find the missing piece of information.

Reflections on the Day

Today students constructed an understanding of a kilowatt-hour and used this understanding to determine how much the value on the meter increases over time depending upon the wattage of a light bulb. They were dealing with two big ideas. The first is that the increase in the number shown on the meter depends upon the number of watts being used. The second is that the wattages used by different appliances can be added together to determine combined power use. Then students played a game based on the relationship of watts, time, and kilowatt-hours.

The Bedtime Mystery

Materials Needed

Weird dials poster (or the meter assembled on Day One)

Student recording sheet for the bedtime mystery investigation (Appendix O)—one per pair of students

Large chart paper—one sheet per pair of students

Markers

Today begins with a continuation of Zig's story. Zig's parents go out in the evening to a movie. Zig is supposed to work on his homework for an hour and then go to bed. The task of the day is to see whether or not Zig turns his light out at 10:00 p.m. In previous investigations students knew the time intervals and the meter readings and used that information to determine the watt ratings of appliances. In this investigation they are told the watt ratings and the meter readings and they have to determine the time the light bulb was turned off—the reverse of the previous process. In solving this mystery, students will be reading, adding, and subtracting decimals. They will also be considering further the relationship between watt-hours and kilowatt-hours. These ideas are discussed in a congress and help develop a deeper understanding of the relationship of place value to decimals.

Day Eight Outline

Developing the Context

☀ Introduce the bedtime mystery investigation and ask students to investigate the scenario described in Appendix O.

Supporting the Investigation

☀ As students work, support them in exploring the relationship between watts and kilowatt-hours.

☀ Be sure students understand that they will need to calculate energy use for the refrigerator and the light separately.

Preparing for the Math Congress

☀ Ask students to prepare posters of the strategies they used and their justifications for their findings.

Facilitating the Math Congress

☀ Facilitate a discussion that will highlight the relationship between watt-hours and kilowatt-hours, ways to find equivalent amounts, and how whole-number computation strategies can be used when computing with decimals.

Developing the Context

Display the weird dials poster (or Appendix A) and tell the following story:

One night Zig's parents go out to a movie. Zig stays home to finish his homework and go to bed. Before his parents leave at 9 p.m., they read the meter. Then they turn off all the lights and appliances in the house, except for the refrigerator and the light in Zig's bedroom. His parents come home at midnight, read the meter, and write down the number. The next morning Zig's father says that he knows what time Zig turned his light out. How does he know?

At this point in the story, ask your students whether they think Zig's father could really figure out the time Zig turned off his light and went to bed. After a preliminary discussion, assign math partners and pass out recording sheets (Appendix O). Ask students to work on the investigation.

☀ Introduce the bedtime mystery investigation and ask students to investigate the scenario described in Appendix O.

Supporting the Investigation

As you circulate and confer with pairs of students, there are two ideas that students should be considering. First, as in the mysteries on Day Seven, students must consider the watt to kilowatt-hour connection. Students may remember from the work on Day Five that the light bulb and refrigerator were described in units of watts (75 for the light bulb and 60 for the refrigerator), but the meter readings are in kilowatt-hours. Other students may remember that the refrigerator uses 0.015 kilowatt-hours every 15 minutes—0.060 kilowatt-hours in an hour. Some students will convert everything to kilowatt-hours and work from there, others will convert the meter's readings into watt-hours since whole numbers are easier to work with, and still others may use combinations of these techniques. It is important to let the pairs work with whichever units they prefer. As you confer with students, however, remind them to keep track of the units they are working in.

Second, the students have to figure out how long Zig's lamp was on. They have to realize that it may or may not have been on as long as the refrigerator was on—the refrigerator was on for the whole time but until the problem is solved, students won't know if this is true of the light. Students will need to calculate energy use for the refrigerator and the light separately. Some students will notice on Appendix O that Zig's father didn't record the tens digit on the meter. This is a nice opportunity to develop some number sense and have students discuss why the value of the tens digit doesn't matter in this problem.

Have the weird dials poster available for students to use. By this point in the unit, most students will not need to use the movable dials, but a few students may still need that support. Some may need a reminder that

☀ As students work, support them in exploring the relationship between watts and kilowatt-hours.

☀ Be sure students understand that they will need to calculate energy use for the refrigerator and the light separately.

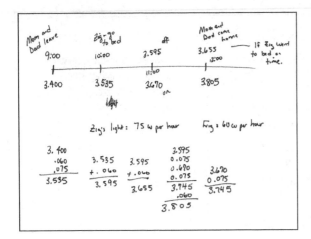

Figure 4a

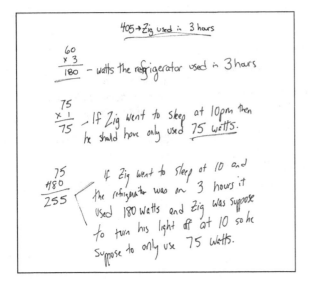

Figure 4b

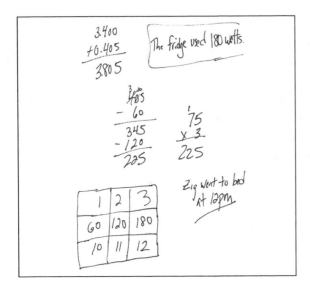

Figure 4c

there are 1000 watt-hours in one kilowatt-hour. If they struggle to convert, help them use a ratio table in the form of a t-chart and work with landmarks. For example,

Watt-hours	Kilowatt-hours
1000	1 or 1.000
500	½ or 0.500
250	¼ or 0.250

The patterns that appear may be sufficient to help them realize that the number of thousandths of kilowatt-hours is the number of watt-hours. Students should find at least eight or ten of these correspondences (watt-hours to kilowatt-hours) to be sure that they see the pattern.

Some students may use number lines to represent the passage of time and indicate the meter readings on the number line (like on a timeline.) *[See Figure 4a]* This is an important representation because it illustrates what one would actually see a meter doing, and it would be very helpful to discuss work of this kind in the math congress. This representation is different from a ratio table that shows kilowatt-hours used over time, because as a timeline it shows the readings of the meter, not the energy used (which is the change in the meter.) That the energy used increases at a steady rate, not the readings themselves, is a big idea for students to construct. Such representation provides a perfect opportunity for the class to discuss how one can use a ratio table, indicating kilowatt-hours used, to create this number line and vice versa.

Depending on the math knowledge levels of your students, this investigation might take more than one class period. Don't rush them! It is important for the students to

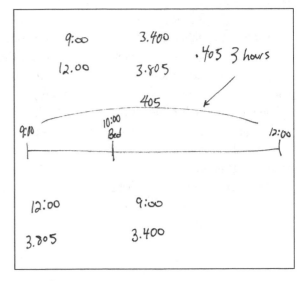

Figure 4d

THE MYSTERY OF THE METER

struggle with the big ideas here. If a pair is struggling, have them talk to another pair of students, before working with them yourself. If they are still confused, remind them of their previous work with the meter. Might that help them solve the mystery? Would a ratio table help?

Preparing for the Math Congress

Have the pairs prepare posters explaining their findings. The students should have a number of ways to have figured out that Zig turned his light out at midnight when his parents arrived at home. (Maybe he was reading a good detective story that he couldn't put down or working on an interesting math problem!) The point of the congress is not to find out what time Zig went to bed, but rather how the students figured out that he stayed up later than he should have. Remember: they are being detectives here, so they have to be able to prove their findings. When most of the students have found a solution and created posters, gather them together for a congress.

Ask students to prepare posters of the strategies they used and their justifications for their findings.

Tips for Structuring the Math Congress

Choose three or four pairs to share their findings. Think about beginning the congress by examining the relationships between kilowatt-hours and watt-hours and ways to find equivalent amounts for kilowatt-hours and watt-hours. Look for pairs who have different methods. Plan next on moving to an examination of posters showing that students worked with different units: for example, a pair who expressed everything as watt-hours and worked with whole numbers versus a pair who expressed everything as kilowatt-hours. Think about structuring the congress to bring out the relationships *between* these methods and imagine a flow of conversation on how the computation strategies used for whole numbers also work for decimals.

Facilitating the Math Congress

Convene the math congress by inviting students to bring their posters to the meeting area. Choose three or four posters that will allow you to have a conversation on the relationship of watt-hours to kilowatt-hours, ways to find equivalent amounts, and how strategies used for computation of whole numbers can be used for decimals. [*See Figures 4a–4d, page 54.*]

During the congress, there may be some confusion between kilowatts and kilowatt-hours. The discussion of watt-hours might even come up. This, in fact, leads to a big idea. The students who work with kilowatt-hours are adding and subtracting decimals, while the students who work with watt-hours are adding and subtracting whole numbers. But the properties of arithmetic they are using are the same! For example, students who increase 3.400 by 0.180 will obtain 3.580, while other students might start with 3400 and add 180 to obtain 3580. If something like this happens, be sure the congress examines what is going on because it captures a big idea involving arithmetic with decimals.

Facilitate a discussion that will highlight the relationship between watt-hours and kilowatt-hours, ways to find equivalent amounts, and how whole-number computation strategies can be used when computing with decimals.

A Portion of the Math Congress

John (the teacher): Kelly and Tina, why don't you tell us what you found out?

Kelly: Well, we started with the fridge. Zig's parents were gone for 3 hours, so the fridge used 180 watt-hours, because 60 plus 60 plus 60 is 180.

Tina: So that would make the meter go to 3.580.

Kevin: What did you do there? I don't understand.

Kelly: We're trying to make the meter go from 3.400 to 3.805 like it did. We added the 180 to 400. So the fridge made it go up to 3.580.

Tina: And for each hour Zig's light was on, it used 75 watt-hours, so we built a chart. *(Points to a chart on their poster.)*

Kelly: If it were on for one hour, the meter would've read 3.655, but that's too low. Two hours would make it 3.730, and three make it 3.805, which is it. So he went to bed at twelve.

John: *(After further conversation ensues on this strategy.)* Ricardo and Tom, you did it a little differently. Would you share how you solved the problem?

Tom: Well, since we knew where the meter started and stopped, we subtracted. That told us how many kilowatt-hours were used.

Ricardo: Which was 0.405 kilowatt-hours or 405 watt-hours.

John: Are you suggesting we could use either? We could use watt-hours or kilowatt-hours? What do people think about this? Turn to the person next to you and discuss this for a few minutes. *(After a few moments of pair talk, conversation resumes.)*

Ricardo: You can because…

Emily: The numbers are the same…well, not really the same. It's sort of like multiplying the kilowatt-hours by 1000 because a kilowatt-hour is 1000 watt-hours. The decimal goes away. But if you want your answer in kilowatt-hours, you have to put the decimal back.

John: And how do we know where to put it? What's happening when you put it back?

continued on next page

Author's Notes

John chooses two pairs: one that has used kilowatt-hours and one that has changed the units to watt-hours.

The students are blending the language of watt-hours and kilowatt-hours here. This shows they are making sense of the relationship between them.

An important point has arisen demanding think time. John focuses reflection on this idea by providing pair talk.

continued from previous page

Tom: Then we're dividing by 1000. Yeah, but we just used watt-hours, because they were easier.

John: Can we use the same kinds of arithmetic strategies that we use with whole numbers?

Questions can also promote reflection. John does not tell students that the same strategies can be used for both decimals and whole numbers. Instead, he encourages them to defend the position.

Ricardo: Yeah. Our way is a little like what Kelly and Tina did. We knew the fridge was on for 3 hours, so we timesed 60 by 3, which means it used 180 watt-hours.

John: Wait, so you multiplied by 3 to find out, but Kelly and Tina, you added, didn't you?

Kelly: Yeah. But it's just the same, because we plussed 75 three times, which is the same as timesing it by 3.

John: Oh, so you both did the same thing?

Reflections on the Day

Today students worked on using the readings of the meter to solve the mystery of Zig's light. In a subsequent math congress they discussed the relationship of watt-hours to kilowatt-hours, ways to find equivalent amounts, and how strategies used for computation of whole numbers can be used for decimals—when adding and subtracting decimals, the calculations work the same way they do with whole numbers.

The Mystery Deepens

Materials Needed

**Weird dials poster
(or the meter assembled
on Day One),** as needed

**Student recording sheet
for the new bedtime
mystery investigation
(Appendix P)**—one per
pair of students

Large chart paper—one
sheet per pair of students

Sticky notes—one pad
per student

Markers

Today students work on a more complex bedtime mystery. The TV and several lights are on and the meter is read at 6:00 P.M. and at 8:00 A.M. In this context students continue to develop fluency in using decimal arithmetic.

Day Nine Outline

Developing the Context

☀ Introduce the new bedtime mystery investigation and have students work in pairs to investigate the questions in Appendix P.

Supporting the Investigation

☀ Encourage students to use ratio tables to help them see the patterns as they work with fractions of an hour.

Preparing for the Math Congress

☀ Ask students to make posters describing how they solved the new bedtime mystery.

☀ Conduct a gallery walk to give students a chance to review and comment on each other's posters.

Facilitating the Math Congress

☀ Facilitate a congress discussion to highlight a range of strategies for doing arithmetic with decimals.

Developing the Context

Today's investigation is an extension of the work undertaken on Day Eight on the bedtime mystery. Explain to students that Zig was surprised that his father was able to determine when he turned off his light by using the meter. Now he wants to try it out for himself. This time Zig read the meter at 6:00 p.m. and again at 8:00 a.m. and he collected data on what appliances and lights were on in the whole house. The television and certain lights were turned on and off. Zig wrote down the times on and off for each.

Pass out recording sheets (Appendix P). Discuss the data on the sheet with students to make sure they understand all components of the context. The two major issues that students need to work on in this investigation are the same as last time: the watt to kilowatt-hour connection and how to figure out how long Zig's light was on. This time, however, the story is more complicated. The students have to deal with more appliances than just the refrigerator and Zig's light bulb. Plus, some appliances are on for fractional portions of hours now. Have students work on this in pairs.

※ Introduce the new bedtime mystery investigation and have students work in pairs to investigate the questions in Appendix P.

Behind the Numbers

In this investigation students have to determine appropriate on and off times for the refrigerator, the TV, Zig's parents' light, and Zig's light. The problem requires that the refrigerator be on the entire time between readings, from 6 P.M. to 8 A.M., the TV be on from 6 P.M. to 8 P.M., and that both Zig's parents' and Zig's lights were turned on at 8 P.M. Although Zig's parents turned their light off at 11:30 P.M., the mystery is when Zig turned off his light. There may be some different interpretations of these on and off times and these will need to be discussed. The numbers are chosen so that it appears Zig's light is turned off at 12 P.M. For this last step, students will have to determine how long a 75-watt bulb is on if it uses 0.300 kilowatt-hours of energy if they worked in kilowatt-hours, or how long it is on if it used 300 watt-hours of energy.

Supporting the Investigation

Some students might still want to use the meter on the weird dials poster. Encourage them to try to solve the problem without spinning the dials, but have the poster available if needed. There may be some confusion about appliances being on for parts of hours. If this occurs, you might ask: "If I have a 100-watt bulb on for one hour, how many kilowatt-hours does it use? What if it was on for two hours? What about half an hour? How do you know?" In this case, a ratio table or t-chart might help students find patterns. If a group has a hard time figuring out when Zig turned off his light, ask how many watt-hours are used by Zig's bulb in fractions of an hour—½ hour, ¼ hour, ⅓ hour, etc. Then ask how that might help them solve the mystery of the light.

※ Encourage students to use ratio tables to help them see the patterns as they work with fractions of an hour.

Preparing for the Math Congress

Provide pairs with chart paper and have them prepare posters describing how they solved the mystery: *What time did Zig turn out his light?* As students work on their posters, walk around and note the computation strategies they are using as they work with decimals. Explain that the class will have a "gallery walk" to look at the posters before starting a math congress. The

※ Ask students to make posters describing how they solved the new bedtime mystery.

※ Conduct a gallery walk to give students a chance to review and comment on each other's posters.

purpose of the gallery walk here is for students to see if there is class agreement on the time Zig went to bed, and to examine the variety of strategies their classmates used. Pass out small pads of sticky notes and suggest that everyone use them to write comments or questions that can then be placed directly onto the posters. Display all the posters around the room and have the students walk around for about fifteen minutes, reading and commenting on the mathematics on each other's posters. Give the students a few minutes to read the comments and questions posted on their own posters and then convene the math congress.

■ Tips for Structuring the Math Congress

Although the type of computations involved in solving this problem are basically the same as in the previous bedtime mystery, there are many components that need to be analyzed (the energy used by the refrigerator, the TV, Zig's parents' light and Zig's light). In addition to developing these components of the problem, also plan on focusing on strategies for doing arithmetic with decimals. [See Figures 5a and 5b.] For example, some students may be using landmark decimals and adding on to get to them. Others may now be using a wide variety of computation strategies that they typically use for whole numbers. In this case, the students are very likely converting to watt-hours for the calculation and then going back to kilowatt-hours. Keep in mind that this is one of the big ideas of the unit, that if the whole is shifted (say from kilowatt-hours to watt-hours) then one can work with decimals using whole number arithmetic. Structure the congress to bring this big idea into the foreground.

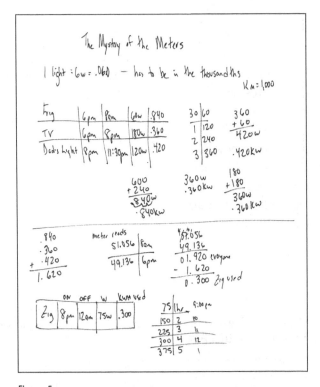

Figure 5a   Figure 5b

Facilitating the Math Congress

After the gallery walk, convene the students in the meeting area for a discussion of the components of the problem as well as a few of the computation strategies used. A focus of the discussion should be on strategies for doing arithmetic with decimals, and the big idea that if the whole is shifted, then one can use whole number arithmetic.

☀ Facilitate a congress discussion to highlight a range of strategies for doing arithmetic with decimals.

Reflections on the Day

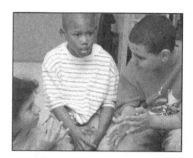

Students worked on a bedtime mystery today as they continued to explore arithmetic strategies with decimals. They held a gallery walk and compared their strategies. This investigation provided them with further experiences and opportunities to develop computation strategies with decimals and in the congress they continued to discuss the big idea that computation with decimals is the same as with whole numbers, if the whole is shifted.

The Real Bedtime and the Cost of Energy for the Television

Materials Needed

Sample electric bill
(Appendix Q)

Student recording sheet
for the bright bulb
mystery investigation
(Appendix R)—one per
pair of students

Large chart paper—two
sheets per pair of students

Sticky notes—one
pad per student

Large chart pad
and easel

Markers

Today begins with a minilesson on equivalent operations. Then students find out that Zig really went to bed at 10 p.m., not 12 p.m. Zig's mother had forgotten to tell him that his bulb had burned out and she had changed it. Students need to find the wattage of Zig's new light bulb. As a challenge, they also work to determine the cost of the energy for the television. A congress is held that continues to focus on arithmetic with decimals in the context of the meter problem.

Day Ten Outline

Minilesson: Equivalent Operations

☀ Conduct a minilesson designed to highlight strategies for multiplying by 25 and by 2.5.

Developing the Context

☀ Introduce the new light bulb and the cost of electricity scenarios and ask students to work in pairs to investigate the questions in Appendix R.

Supporting the Investigation

☀ As students work on the cost of electricity problem, remind them of their work in today's minilesson and encourage them to consider the relationship between kilowatt-hours and watt-hours.

Preparing for the Math Congress

☀ Ask students to prepare posters of their work and then conduct a gallery walk.

Facilitating the Math Congress

☀ Facilitate a congress discussion to highlight different computation strategies for working with decimals.

☀ Pose and discuss a series of computation problems designed to help students choose strategies that make sense, given the numbers in the problems.

Minilesson: Equivalent Operations (10-15 minutes)

This string of multiplication and division problems requires students to think about strategies for multiplying by 25 and by 2.5. Do one problem at a time and ask students to give a thumbs-up when they know the answer. After sufficient think time, ask a few students to explain their reasoning, and when possible, represent their strategies. Explore a variety of strategies for solving the same problem and have students compare them. Then move to the next question. As you proceed through the string, facilitate a discussion on how the problems in the string are related.

☀ Conduct a minilesson designed to highlight strategies for multiplying by 25 and by 2.5.

Behind the Numbers

To multiply by 25, students can divide by 4 and multiply by 100. Many students will use a monetary model to think about this. A similar strategy for multiplying by 2.5 is to divide by 4 and multiply by 10. Finally, multiplying by 0.25 is the same as dividing by 4. This is because 0.25 is equivalent to $\frac{1}{4}$. Again students will probably use a monetary model (25 cents = $\frac{1}{4}$ dollar) to make sense of this. The numbers in this string were chosen to encourage students to notice and use these relationships. At first, don't expect students to make use of the relationships. As you proceed through the string, however, they will notice the relationships in the answers and you can then facilitate a productive discussion on the relationships.

String of related problems:

$$4 \times 25$$
$$8 \times 25$$
$$8 \div 4$$
$$32 \div 4$$
$$32 \times 25$$
$$2 \times 2.5$$
$$20 \times 2.5$$
$$20 \div 4$$
$$44 \div 4$$
$$44 \times 25$$
$$44 \times 2.5$$
$$44 \times 0.25$$

Assessment Tips

It is helpful to keep a pad of sticky notes or some index cards near you when you do strings. If you can, jot down notes as you see students use interesting strategies and develop flexibility with computation. Use one sticky note or card for each student. At the end of the day, you can copy the string, attach your note, and place it in the student's portfolio. Make notes about the strategies and big ideas described in the introduction to this unit (pages 7–9).

Developing the Context

☀ Introduce the new light bulb and the cost of electricity scenarios and ask students to work in pairs to investigate the questions in Appendix R.

Two challenges are provided to students today; they can work on one or both. For the first, continue with Zig's story:

Zig is very surprised to learn that his calculations show he had gone to bed at midnight! He didn't. He went to bed at 10 P.M. and he remembered to turn his light off! Zig checks his arithmetic and at first can't figure out where the mistake is. Then he notices that his light bulb seems extra bright and he asks his mother about it. She says she forgot to tell him that she had changed his light bulb the other day.

Figuring out the wattage of the new light bulb is one investigation.

A second investigation relates to the cost of electricity. Although the cost varies from community to community, in this problem the cost is $0.25 per kilowatt-hour. You can display the sample electric bill in Appendix Q as you develop this context. Zig wonders if it costs a lot to have a bright light bulb in his room. His mother says, "Not as much as watching TV costs." She asks him to figure out how much energy the television would require if it were on for 100 hours.

Distribute recording sheets (Appendix R) and have the students work in pairs.

Behind the Numbers

The price for electricity is based upon kilowatt-hours used (although there are other fees in the bill as well). The price of electricity varies across the country and the price in your community may be less than $0.25 per kilowatt-hour; this number was chosen for this investigation because it is a landmark number and it is connected to the work done in the minilesson. Finding the cost of electricity for a 180-watt television that is on for 100 hours emphasizes place value with decimals, as students will need to calculate 180 watts x 100 hours x $0.25 (per kilowatt). They will need to consider the relationship between kilowatt-hours and watt-hours again: 18,000 watt-hours = 18 kilowatt-hours.

Determining the answer to the new light bulb problem can be done with the work of Day Nine. The 75-watt bulb uses 300 watt-hours in four hours and if that type bulb was used, then Zig must have had his light on from 8:00 to midnight. What kind of bulb would have burned the 300 watt-hours in two hours? A 150-watt bulb will burn 300 watt-hours in two hours.

Supporting the Investigation

☀ As students work on the cost of electricity problem, remind them of their work in today's minilesson and encourage them to consider the relationship between kilowatt-hours and watt-hours.

The problem of finding the price of electricity for the refrigerator for one day's use is a new type of question. If students have difficulty, keep them grounded in the context. Remind them that it is the electric meter that is read, and when the value on the meter increases by 1 kilowatt-hour the charge will be 25 cents. So 2 kilowatt-hours cost 50 cents, 4 cost a dollar, and so forth. The minilesson was designed to support this type of computation, but students may need to grapple with the concept of place value in order to solve the price problem.

Preparing for the Math Congress

After a sufficient amount of time, ask students to prepare posters of their work. Set up two displays, one for each investigation. Have a gallery walk and note the strategies used. Some students may have added kilowatt-hour usage, one hour at a time, to find the total energy used. Others may have used the watts provided and multiplied by the number of hours and then converted to kilowatt-hours. Some students may never convert to kilowatt-hours. These strategies should be noted because they will reintroduce a big idea from the bedtime mystery congress on Day Eight: that arithmetic with decimals is the same as with whole numbers, except that students have to find equivalences for different units (in this case, watt-hours and kilowatt-hours.) Regarding the problem of the price of the energy needed to run the television, look for strategies that will demonstrate the choice to compute with decimals.

☀ Ask students to prepare posters of their work and then conduct a gallery walk.

Facilitating the Math Congress

Begin the congress by having a few groups share their strategies for finding energy used by the various appliances. Compare work done in kilowatt-hours with work done in watt-hours. Ask students to tell how the computations are similar and how they are different. Keep the discussions short. The main focus here is on the different computation strategies that can be used for working with decimals. After this discussion, pose the following questions:

> *Suppose I want to calculate 4.225 × 3. What do I do? What if it was 4225 × 3?*
>
> *Suppose I want to calculate 13.773 − 13.663? What do I do? What if I calculated 773 − 663? How does this help?*

Have students engage in pair talk about the following question:

> *Suppose I am calculating with decimals and I forget about the decimal point. What can happen?*

After discussing responses, pose two more questions for pair talk and subsequent discussion:

> *Suppose I needed to calculate 4.5 + 2.25?*
>
> *Suppose I needed to calculate 3.25 − 3.025?*

☀ Facilitate a congress discussion to highlight different computation strategies for working with decimals.

☀ Pose and discuss a series of computation problems designed to help students choose strategies that make sense, given the numbers in the problems.

Behind the Numbers

The purpose of the numbers in these questions is to push students to make sense of the quantities and to choose a strategy that makes sense. It is not to encourage students to say, "I need to use pencil and paper and line the numbers up!" The problem 4.5 + 2.25 can be thought of as 6 + 0.75; 3.25 − 3.025 can be thought of as 250 − 25 and then rewritten into decimal form. Encourage flexibility!

Reflections on the Unit

Thomas Edison said, "Just because something doesn't do what you planned it to do doesn't mean it's useless" (www.quotedb.com /quotes/1378). When mathematics is understood as mathematizing one's world—interpreting, organizing, inquiring about, and constructing meaning through a mathematical lens— it becomes creative and alive. Mysteries, and even one's mistakes, can be sources of insight.

Traditionally mathematics has been taught in our schools as if it were a dead language. It was something that mathematicians had developed in the past—something that needed to be learned, practiced, and applied. When the definition of mathematics shifts toward the activity of mathematizing one's lived world, the constructive nature of the discipline and its connection to problem solving become clear.

In this unit, students were invited to find ways to mathematize situations in their own lived worlds. They explored mysteries involving electric meters, the relationships between the spinning hands on dials, the energy uses of appliances, and the time at which Zig went to bed. They constructed an understanding of place value with decimals and formulated various strategies for calculating with them. Within all these rich contexts, students were developing several big ideas, strategies, and important models for decimals. They also worked hard on strategies for efficient computation with decimals and explored how decimals are related to multiplication and division by powers of ten.

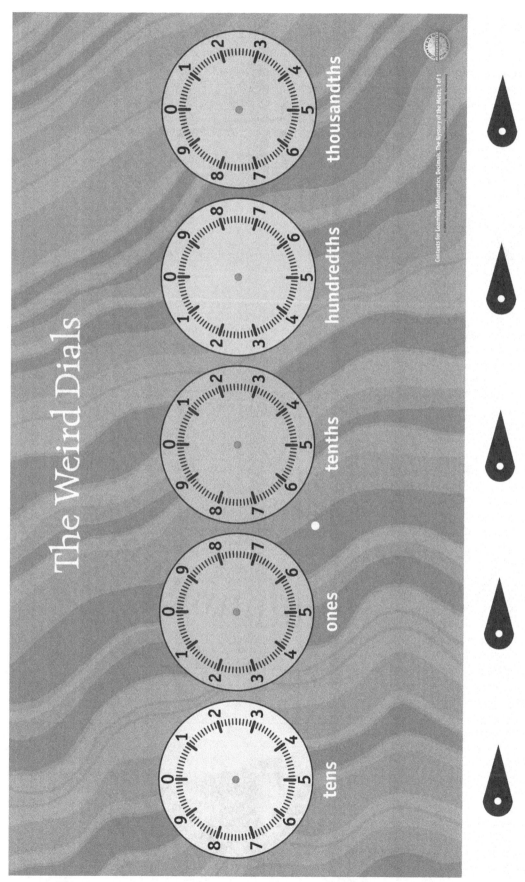

■ To assemble a weird dials poster, make 5 copies of this page and number three dials clockwise and two dials counter-clockwise. Glue the dials on cardboard alternating the directions of rotation as in the meter in Appendix B and attach a hand to the center of each dial with a thumbtack. Under each dial indicate "tens", "ones", "tenths", hundredths", or "thousandths" (as shown on page 68).

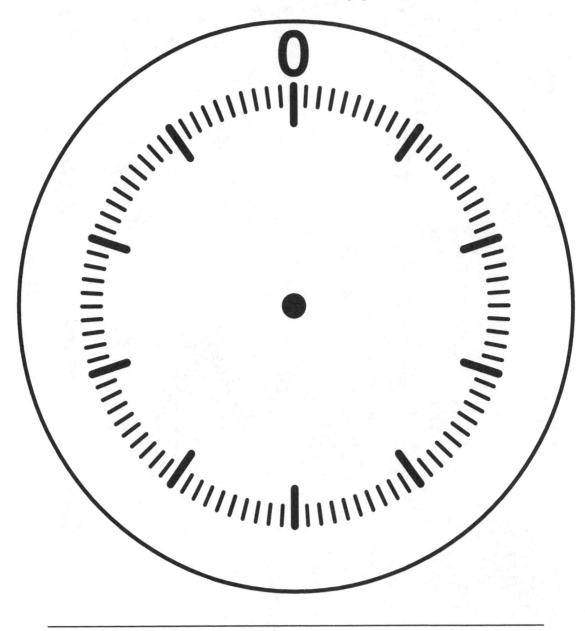

Zig is playing behind his house one day and finds a weird series of dials. This is what he sees:

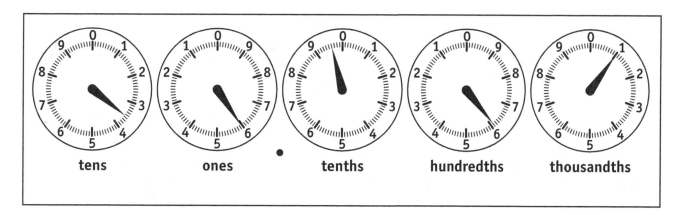

| tens | ones | tenths | hundredths | thousandths |

What do you notice about these dials?
What do you think they show?

Appendix C   Student recording sheet for the weird dials investigation

Names _____ Date _____

Zig's notes:

I noticed that the hands move. I will watch really carefully and every ten minutes I will draw a picture and record what the dials show.

Here are my results. Wow! I think I am beginning to see how the dials are related.

What do you think Zig means? How do you think the hands on the dials move? If you were to write down numbers for what you see, what would you write?

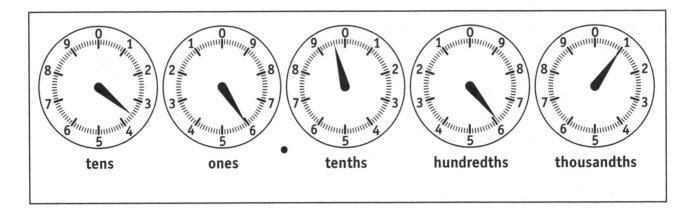

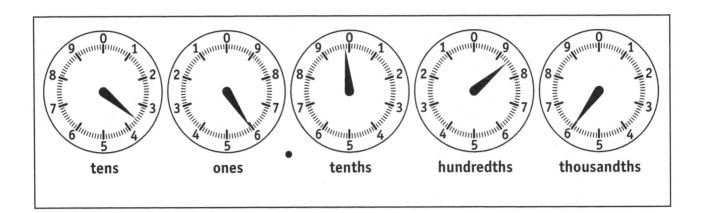

THE MYSTERY OF THE METER

Appendix C

Student recording sheet for the weird dials investigation

Names _____ Date _____

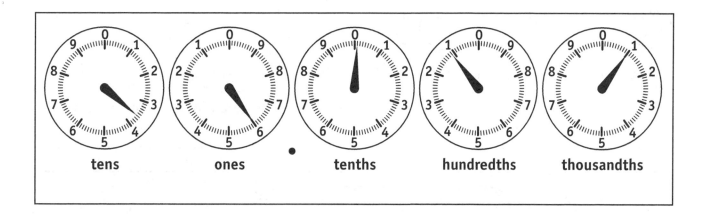

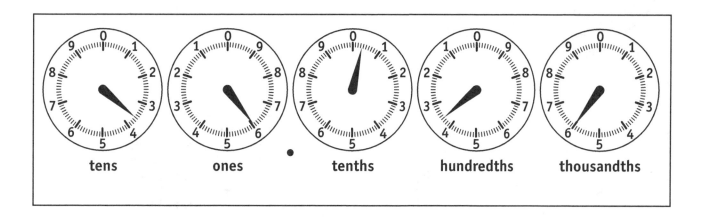

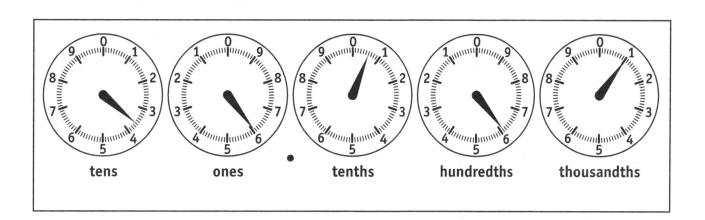

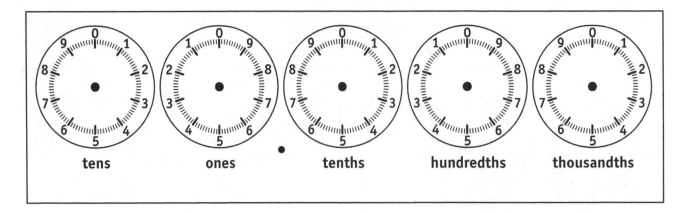

tens   ones   tenths   hundredths   thousandths

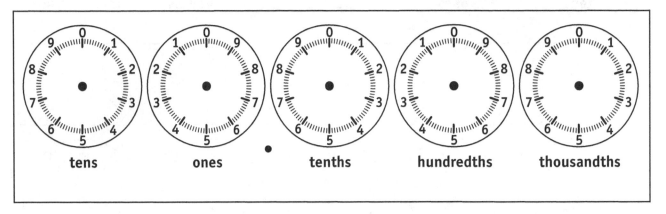

tens   ones   tenths   hundredths   thousandths

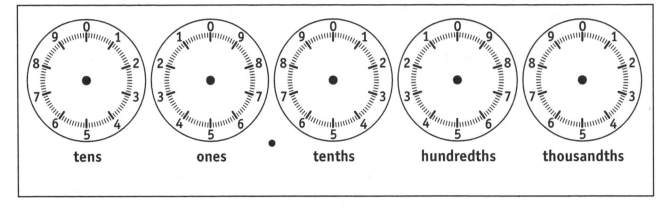

tens   ones   tenths   hundredths   thousandths

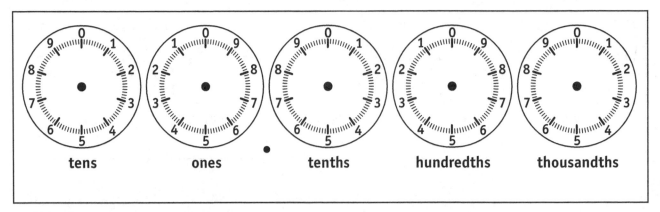

tens   ones   tenths   hundredths   thousandths

Names _____ Date _____

How do you think the movement of the hand on one of the dials makes the hands on the other dials move?

Suppose the hand on the hundredths dial spins ten times. What happens to the hand on the tenths dial? What happens to the hand on the thousandths dial? How do you know?

Suppose the hand on the ones dial spins 45 times. What happens to the hands on all the other dials?

Suppose the hand on the tenths dial spins $135\frac{1}{2}$ times. What happens to the hands on the other dials?

Make up your own question about the dials.

Appendix F   Student recording sheet for the neighborhood meters investigation

Zig learns from his father that the meter measures electric energy use in kilowatt-hours and that a diesel-electric train uses 5000 kilowatts at full speed. This means that if the train had a similar meter the ones dial would spin 5000 times in one hour.

Here is Zig's meter in the morning. He recorded 46.025. His father tells him he has read it correctly.

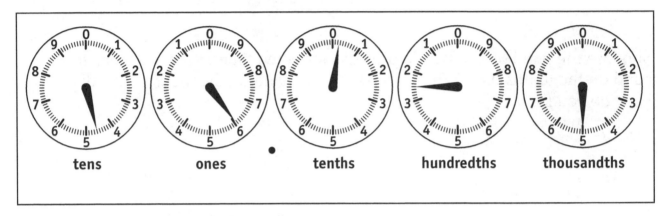

Suppose you are a meter reader. You have the same problem that Zig does. Some of the dials are covered by bushes and you can't see them all.

1. Is it possible to read a meter if you cannot see all the dials?
2. If so, what are the readings for the following meters? Try to find out.

Osgood

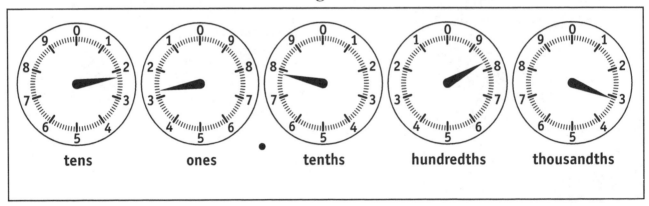

THE MYSTERY OF THE METER

Appendix F   Student recording sheet for the neighborhood meters investigation

Sanchez

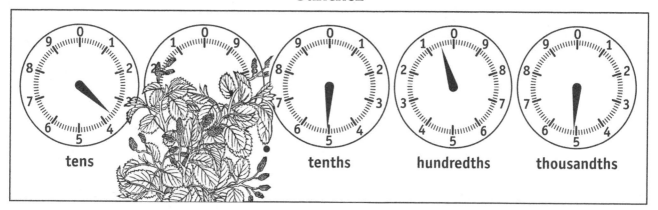

Jones

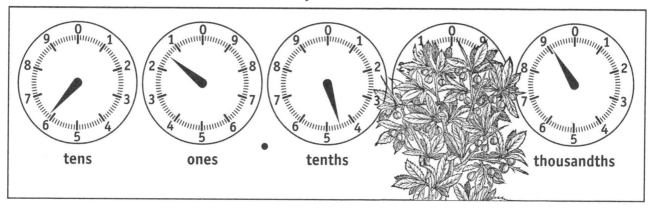

Hilbert

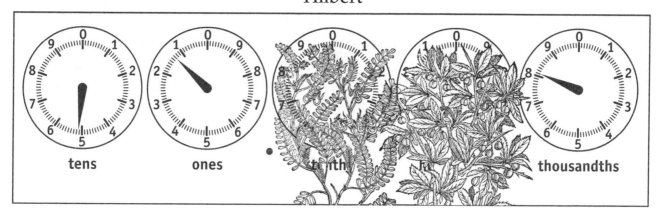

Hsaing

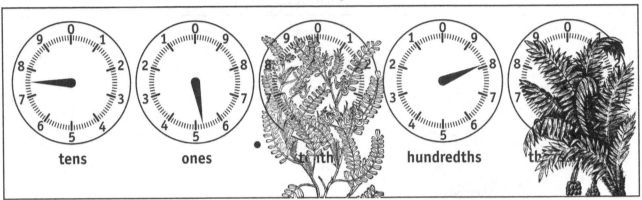

tens   ones   tenth   hundredths   th

Now draw a different meter. Challenge your classmates.

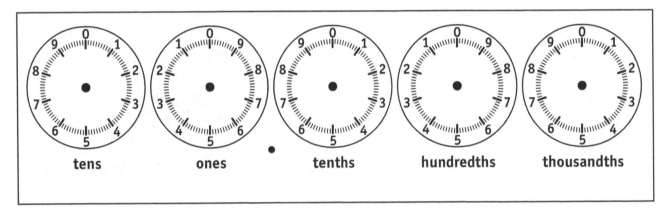

tens   ones   tenths   hundredths   thousandths

What does your meter read?

How many dials can be missing yet still allow you to read a meter?
Support your assertion with convincing reasons.

The following is the rule Zig devised:

First, for each dial where you can see the hand, write down the greatest number that the hand has just passed. Make sure you go in the correct direction! If you can't see the number, leave a blank space. To fill in the blank, look at the dial on the left and count the number of dashes from its number until they come up to the hand. Put that number in the blank space.

Zig shows his parents the following rule for reading meters that are missing a dial:

First, for each dial where you can see the hand, write down the greatest number that the hand has just passed. Make sure you go in the correct direction! If you can't see the number, leave a blank space. To fill in the blank, look at the dial on the left and count the number of dashes from its number until they come up to the hand. Put that number in the blank space.

Is Zig's rule a good rule for reading meters that have hidden dials?

Is it similar to the rules considered in class?

Does it need some modifying?

Dedekind

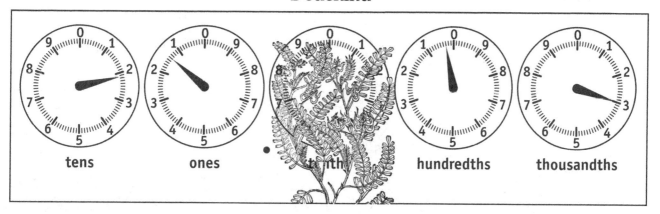

Kummer

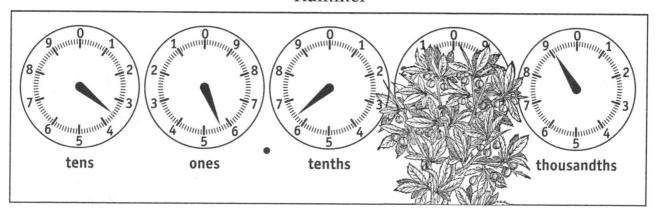

Fermat

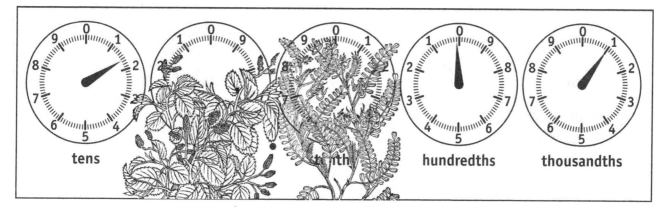

Experiment #1

Zig decides to experiment. He believes he has turned off all the lights and all the appliances in the house. He goes outside and reads the meter three times, 15 minutes apart. Here is what he finds:

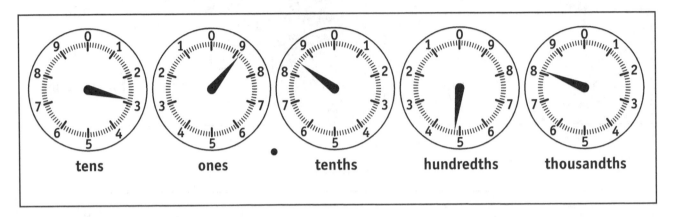

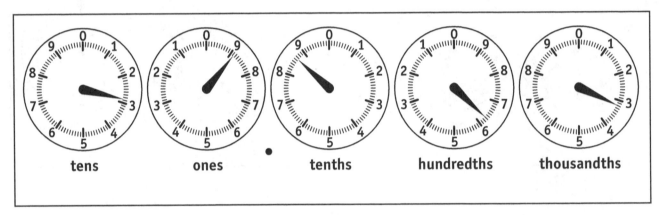

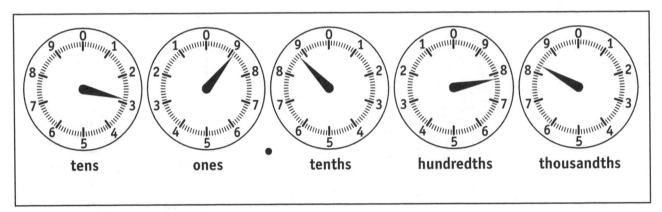

Zig is very perplexed. What do you think happened?

Appendix J

gon reasoning

Experiment #2

Zig goes inside and sits on the couch, pondering his meter readings. He sits very quietly for a long time, perplexed by the meter readings. He then hears a humming sound. What's that? There isn't anybody in the house and all the lights are out. Finally he realizes that the humming sound is coming from the refrigerator. He didn't turn off the refrigerator! Zig unplugs the refrigerator and here is what he finds, again reading the meter three times, 15 minutes apart:

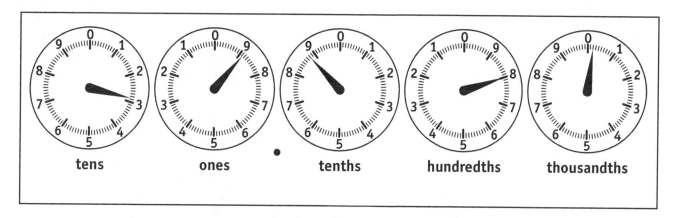

tens ones tenths hundredths thousandths

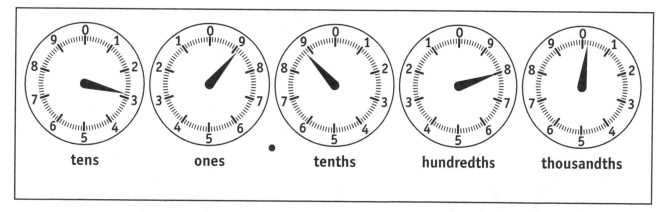

tens ones tenths hundredths thousandths

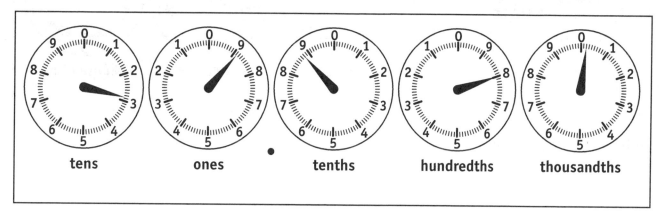

tens ones tenths hundredths thousandths

What happened?

Experiment #3

Now Zig goes to the living room. He turns on a light there, which he knows is 100 watts. He checks the meter three more times, 15 minutes apart.

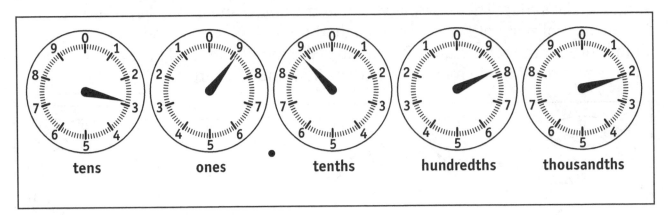

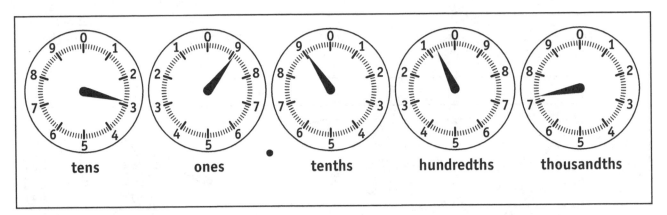

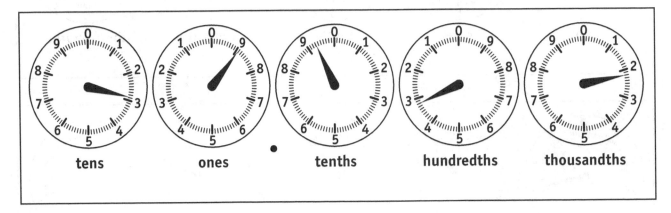

What does this mean?

Experiment #4

Then Zig remembered that he had better plug the refrigerator back in! He goes back and completes three more readings, again 15 minutes apart. Here is what he found.

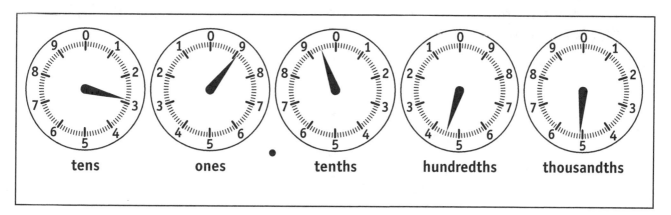

tens   ones   tenths   hundredths   thousandths

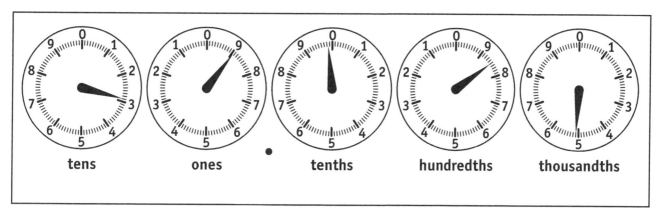

tens   ones   tenths   hundredths   thousandths

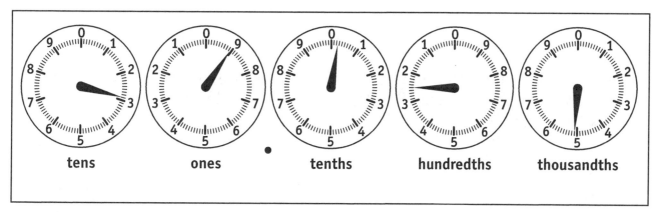

tens   ones   tenths   hundredths   thousandths

Now Zig has a real mystery. He knows that the light bulb in the living room has 100 marked on it. But what do all these dial changes mean?

Zig decides to complete some more experiments. Here is what he finds.

1. With the refrigerator off and all lights off except his bedroom light, he reads the meter every 20 minutes. The readings are 31.355, 31.380, 31.405, and 31.430. What is the wattage of his bedroom light bulb?

2. With only the refrigerator and the kitchen light on, Zig reads the meter every 30 minutes. The readings are 31.825, 31.885, and 31.945. What is the wattage of the kitchen lightbulb?

Appendix L

■ These cards can be made more durable by pasting them on oaktag and laminating them.

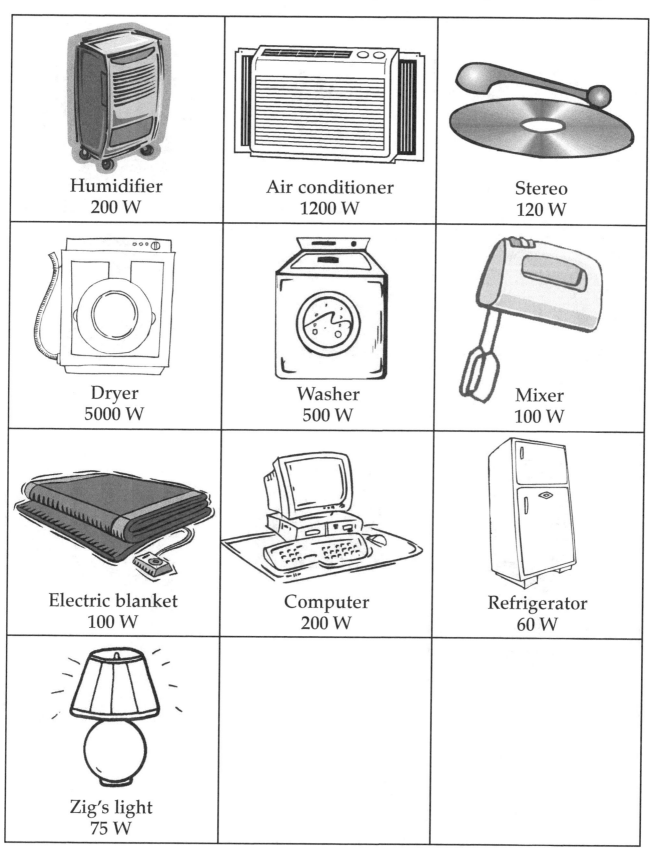

Humidifier 200 W	Air conditioner 1200 W	Stereo 120 W
Dryer 5000 W	Washer 500 W	Mixer 100 W
Electric blanket 100 W	Computer 200 W	Refrigerator 60 W
Zig's light 75 W		

■ These cards can be made more durable by pasting them on oaktag and laminating them.

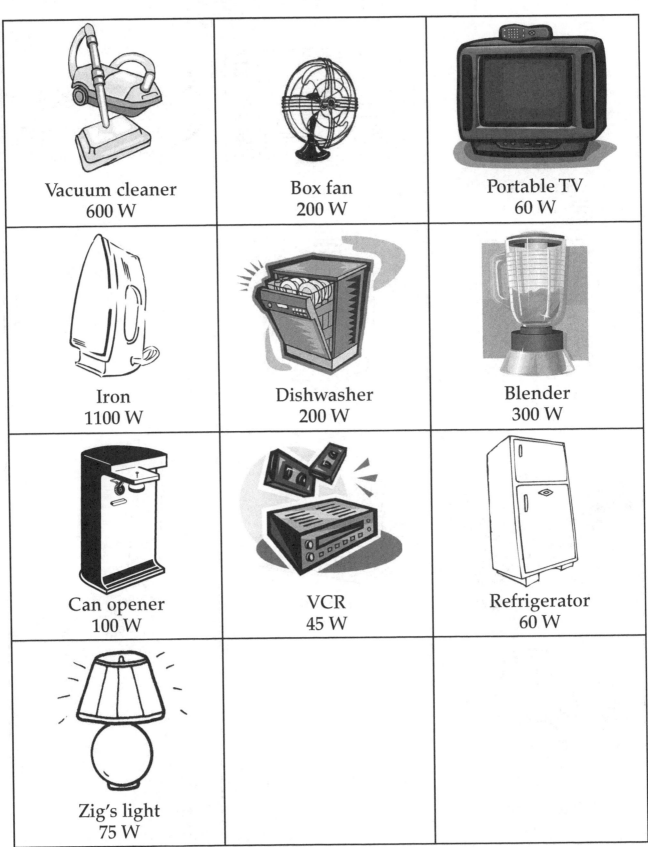

Vacuum cleaner 600 W	Box fan 200 W	Portable TV 60 W
Iron 1100 W	Dishwasher 200 W	Blender 300 W
Can opener 100 W	VCR 45 W	Refrigerator 60 W
Zig's light 75 W		

■ These cards can be made more durable by pasting them on oaktag and laminating them.

Aquarium heater 100 W	**Radio** 75 W	**Oven** 4000 W
Bread maker 680 W	**Deep fryer** 1500 W	**Refrigerator** 60 W
Zig's light 75 W		

■ These cards can be made more durable by pasting them on oaktag and laminating them.

30 minutes	1 hour	2 hours
3 hours	4 hours	5 hours
	8 hours	

■ These cards can be made more durable by pasting them on oaktag and laminating them.

10 minutes	15 minutes	20 minutes
30 minutes	45 minutes	

■ These cards can be made more durable by pasting them on oaktag and laminating them.

20 minutes	40 minutes	80 minutes
90 minutes	100 minutes	24 hours

Student recording sheet for the Meter Reader game

Date _____

Round___

Customers: _____

Meter Readers: _____

Initial Reading: _____ Final Reading: _____

Appliance and wattage: _____ Time: _____

Winners of the Round: _____

Round___

Customers: _____

Meter Readers: _____

Initial Reading: _____ Final Reading: _____

Appliance and wattage: _____ Time: _____

Winners of the Round: _____

Round___

Customers: _____

Meter Readers: _____

Initial Reading: _____ Final Reading: _____

Appliance and wattage: _____ Time: _____

Winners of the Round: _____

Names _____   Date _____

Zig's parents leave to go see a movie at 9 p.m. Zig stays home to finish his homework, then turns out his 75-watt light, and goes to bed by 10 p.m. Before Zig's father leaves, he checks the meter to find out that it reads 3.400 kilowatt-hours.

When Zig's parents come home at midnight, his father checks the meter again and it reads 3.805 kilowatt-hours. The 60-watt refrigerator was the only thing on during their time away, other than Zig's light. Did Zig turn his light off at 10 p.m.? How do you know?

Appendix P   Student recording sheet for the new bedtime mystery investigation

Names _____ Date _____

Here's what happened that night:

All night, the refrigerator was on.

Zig and his parents watched TV together from 6 p.m. to 8 p.m.

Afterward, his parents read from 8 p.m. until 11:30 p.m.

At 8 p.m. Zig said goodnight to his parents and went to his bedroom to read. He turned his light off just before he went to bed.

Here's a chart that Zig made. Is this enough information to solve the mystery of when Zig went to bed?

Appliance	Wattage	Turned On	Turned Off	kWh Used
Refrigerator	60 W			
TV	180 W			
Parents' lights	120 W			
Zig's light	75 W			

The meter read 49.136 at 6 p.m. and then read 51.056 at 8 a.m. the next morning.

What time did Zig go to bed? How do you know?

	KWH	ADT
DEC 06	992	40
NOV 06	1041	48
OCT 06	1407	55
SEP 06	1460	64
AUG 06	1452	72
JUL 06	1397	73
JUN 06	1545	61
MAY 06	779	50
APR 06	842	43
MAR 06	846	29
FEB 06	926	33
JAN 06	1310	29
DEC 05	859	33

APPROXIMATE NEXT METER READING: 1/15/07

METER NUMBER	METER READING PREVIOUS	PRESENT	NUMBER OF DAYS	METER CONSTANT	METERED USAGE	METERED DEMAND	RATE CODE
37436	24913	25905	29		992.00 KWH		D

LAST BILL AMOUNT   161.90
PAYMENTS THROUGH 12/18/06 THANK YOU   161.90CR
BALANCE FORWARD $.00

CURRENT CHARGES   ELECTRIC SERVICE   SERVICE PERIOD 11/17/06-12/16/06
DELIVERY SERVICES RESIDENTIAL

	METER CONSTANT		METERED USAGE	
Customer Chg				8.40
Delivery Chg-First 250KWH	250.00 KWH	x	$.02784	6.96
Delivery Chg-Over 250 KWH	742.00 KWH	x	$.03282	24.35
Stranded Cost Chg	992.00 KWH	x	$.00631	6.26
TAXES & SURCHARGES				
System Benefits Chg	992.00 KWH	x	$.00300	2.98
Consumption Tax	992.00 KWH	x	$.00055	.55
TOTAL CURRENT EL CHARGES				$49.50

CURRENT CHARGES   SUPPLIER SVC EL   SERVICE PERIOD 11/17/06-12/16/06

	METER CONSTANT		METERED USAGE	
Energy Service - Fixed	992.00 KWH	x	$.11264	111.74
TOTAL CURRENT SS CHARGES				$111.74

TOTAL AMOUNT DUE $161.24

Names _____ Date _____

Zig is puzzled. His calculations show that he went to bed at midnight. But he knows that he went to bed at 10 p.m. He checks his arithmetic but can't figure out what's wrong. Then he notices that the light bulb in his room seems brighter than before, and he learns that his mother had replaced his 75-watt bulb with a higher-watt bulb.

If Zig really did go to bed at 10 p.m., what is the wattage of the new light bulb?

Electricity costs $0.25 per kilowatt-hour at Zig's house. Zig's television uses 180 watts. How much does Zig's television cost to run for 100 hours?